best
hikes
with
dogs
ARIZONA

best hikes with dogs ARIZONA

Renée Guillory

THE MOUNTAINEERS BOOKS

Dedication

For everyone working to protect beloved places or to improve the
quality of life for animals, thank you.

THE MOUNTAINEERS BOOKS
*is the nonprofit publishing arm of The Mountaineers Club, an organization
founded in 1906 and dedicated to the exploration, preservation, and
enjoyment of outdoor and wilderness areas.*

1001 SW Klickitat Way, Suite 201, Seattle, WA 98134

First edition, 2004

Published simultaneously in Great Britain by Cordee, 3a DeMontfort Street, Leicester,
England, LE1 7HD

Manufactured in Canada

Acquiring Editor: Cassandra Conyers
Project Editor: Laura Drury
Copy Editor: Erin Moore
Cover and Book Design: The Mountaineers Books
Layout: Mayumi Thompson
Cartographer: Moore Creative Designs and Judy Petry
All photographs by author unless otherwise noted

Cover photograph: Getty Images
Frontispiece: *Blue frolicking in Wilson Canyon.* Renée Guillory

Maps shown in this book were produced using National Geographic's *TOPO!*
software. For more information, go to *www.nationalgeographic.com/topo.*

Library of Congress Cataloging-in-Publication Data
Guillory, Renée.
  Best hikes with dogs. Arizona / Renée Guillory.— 1st ed.
    p. cm.
  Includes index.
  ISBN 0-89886-969-2
  1. Hiking with dogs—Arizona—Guidebooks. 2. Trails—Arizona—Guidebooks. 3.
Arizona—Guidebooks. I. Title: Arizona. II. Title.
  SF427.455.G85 2005
  796.51'09791—dc22
                                    2004020868

CONTENTS

Mogollon Rim Country

Central and Western Arizona

Mazatzal Mountains and Area

Phoenix Area Urban Parks

Black Mesa and Perry Mesa

Prescott Area

Sierra Ancha Forest

Western Deserts

Southern and Eastern Arizona

Border Country

Dragoon Mountains

Santa Rita Mountains

Santa Catalina Mountains and Area

The White Mountains

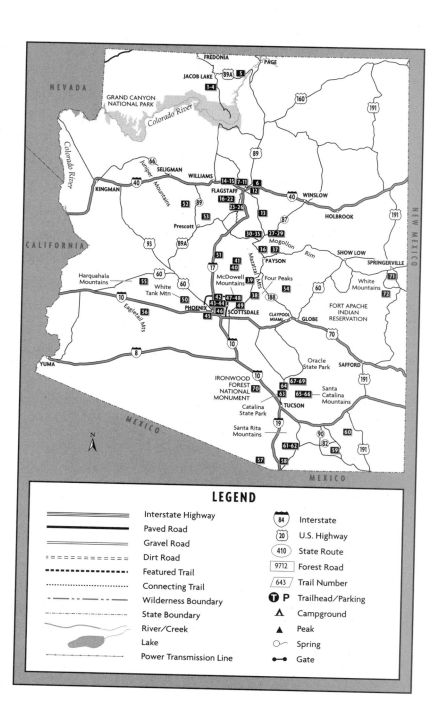

LEGEND

Interstate Highway	Interstate
Paved Road	U.S. Highway
Gravel Road	State Route
Dirt Road	Forest Road
Featured Trail	Trail Number
Connecting Trail	Trailhead/Parking
Wilderness Boundary	Campground
State Boundary	Peak
River/Creek	Spring
Lake	Gate
Power Transmission Line	

HIKE SUMMARY TABLE

Trail	Easy on paws	4 miles or less	Possible overnight trip	Access to perennial stream	Ephemeral stream(s), spring(s), or lake(s)	Unleashed okay	Solitude	Alpine scenery	Forested trail for much of the hike	Good for senior dogs	Best for well conditioned dogs
1 Rainbow Rim to North Timp Point	●		●		●	●			●	●	
2 Lookout Canyon 120	●		●		●	●			●	●	
3 Lookout Canyon 121	●		●		●	●	●		●	●	
4 Lookout Canyon 122	●	●	●		●	●	●		●	●	
5 Sun Valley	●	●			●	●	●			●	
6 Rio de Flag South	●	●			●				●	●	
7 Buffalo Park Urban Loop	●	●			●					●	
8 Little Spring to Bismarck Lake	●	●			●		●	●	●	●	
9 Walker Lake	●	●			●		●	●	●	●	
10 Red Mountain	●	●			●					●	
11 Weatherford	●		●		●		●	●	●		●
12 Sandys Canyon to Walnut Canyon	●				●		●			●	
13 Hutch Mtn. to Gooseberry Spring		●			●		●	●	●	●	
14 Route 66	●	●							●	●	
15 Keyhole Sink	●	●			●				●	●	
16 Sycamore Rim Loop	●				●					●	
17 Sycamore Basin	●				●		●			●	
18 Geronimo Spring	●	●	●		●		●			●	●
19 Dorsey Spring	●		●		●		●		●	●	
20 Hog Hill to Winter Cabin Spring	●		●		●		●		●	●	
21 Parsons Spring	●			●						●	
22 Huckaby	●	●		●	●					●	
23 Margs Draw	●	●			●					●	
24 Vultee Arch	●	●			●				●	●	

Trail	Easy on paws	4 miles or less	Possible overnight trip	Access to perennial stream	Ephemeral stream(s), spring(s), or lake(s)	Unleashed okay	Solitude	Alpine scenery	Forested trail for much of the hike	Good for senior dogs	Best for well conditioned dogs
25 Wilson Canyon	•	•			•					•	•
26 Secret Mountain	•				•		•			•	•
27 Macks Crossing	•	•		•		•				•	
28 Horse Crossing	•	•		•			•			•	•
29 Houston Brothers to Aspen Spring	•	•	•		•		•			•	•
30 Pivot Rock Canyon	•	•	•		•		•			•	•
31 Wildcat Spring	•	•	•		•		•			•	•
32 Calloway		•		•			•			•	•
33 Maxwell		•		•			•			•	•
34 Fossil Springs	•		•	•	•		•				•
35 Deadman Mesa			•	•	•	•	•				•
36 Red Rock Spring	•	•			•		•			•	•
37 Horton Creek	•			•	•					•	•
38 Four Peaks Loop	•	•					•				•
39 Little Saddle Mountain					•		•				•
40 Cave Creek	•			•			•			•	
41 Verde River from Sheep Bridge	•	•		•	•		•			•	
42 Lookout Mountain Summit		•									•
43 North Mountain National	•	•								•	
44 Mohave		•								•	
45 Ranger		•								•	
46 West Park Loop	•	•		•						•	
47 Lousley Hill		•								•	
48 Wagner Loop	•			•						•	
49 Wind Cave	•	•								•	

Trail	Easy on paws	4 miles or less	Possible overnight trip	Access to perennial stream	Ephemeral stream(s), spring(s), or lake(s)	Unleashed okay	Solitude	Alpine scenery	Forested trail for much of the hike	Good for senior dogs	Best for well conditioned dogs
50 Waterfall Canyon	•	•			•					•	
51 Agua Fria National Monument	•	•		•		•	•				•
52 Oaks and Willows	•				•		•			•	•
53 Woodchute	•						•			•	
54 Parker Creek	•				•		•		•	•	
55 Harquahala Mountain Summit			•		•	•	•				•
56 Ben Avery to Indian Spring	•				•	•	•			•	
57 Sycamore Canyon	•			•			•				•
58 Sonoita Creek	•	•		•						•	
59 San Pedro River	•			•		•	•			•	
60 Cochise Stronghold	•				•		•			•	
61 Gardner Canyon	•			•	•		•		•		•
62 Super	•				•						•
63 Romero Canyon to Montrose Pools	•	•			•					•	
64 Sutherland	•				•					•	
65 Butterfly to Crystal Spring	•				•		•		•		•
66 Green Mtn. to Maverick Spring	•				•		•		•	•	
67 Arizona Trail to High Jinks		•			•		•			•	
68 Mariposa		•			•		•			•	
69 Arizona Trail at Oracle					•		•			•	
70 Ironwood Forest Nat'l Monument		•			•		•			•	
71 South Fork	•			•	•		•	•	•	•	
72 Indian Spring Loop	•				•		•	•		•	

ACKNOWLEDGMENTS

To the land managers who offered thoughtful comments on the trail write-ups and who shared their own insights about hiking with dogs goes my enormous gratitude.

The editors and designers at The Mountaineers Books are terrific collaborators—thanks especially to Laura Drury, Erin Moore, and Mayumi Thompson for their patient guidance throughout this project.

Wows and *milles mercis* to Ann Polk, always on call with wit, friendship, and support, including but not limited to administrative help that was crucial to this book—a lifetime supply of chocolate would not be adequate recompense, but it's a start, right? Thanks to Nanny, for *Ranger Rick Magazine* and countless readings of "The Snow Queen," a tale that fed my wanderlust; and to my mother and father, who still root for me and always encouraged my love of the outdoors.

Thanks to those who inspire and challenge me: Sandy Bahr, for her dedication to wild places (and for making the call); Regina Marler, for sharing her passion and respect for the written word – and for so patiently guiding mine; and Elizabeth Pietrzak, for recollections of Duchess and keen commentary.

Gracias to Stef Haslam: you helped make Artemis the wonderful trail dog she is, and you found Dr. Mark Halver, who cares for our animals so lovingly and always makes time for questions.

Finally, thanks to Ken Sweat and our dogs Artemis and Sparky—they learned new definitions for patience and are troupers all . . . and to my cat Puck, who hopes that the not-at-all-anticipated "Best Hikes with Cats" series will come next.

Opposite: Desert wash, near Oracle

INTRODUCTION

It gives me tremendous joy to watch my three-year-old Akita-Collie mix, Artemis, discover a place, her almost prehensile nose crinkling wildly, her curled tail on auto-wag. My twelve-year-old Husky mix, Sparky, has a somewhat different personality on the trail, but one just as amenable to hiking: she is a true slogger, machine-like in her desire to get there—wherever "there" is—happy to be rambling, and friendly and calm with anyone we meet. I am fortunate to have been able to enjoy so many outdoor experiences with these trail-hardy family dogs.

Hiking with Your Dog

When we take dogs hiking, we are not just keeping ourselves company, we are also giving our dogs fun outings and helping them to stay healthier by keeping them physically conditioned. It is tempting to think of outdoor adventure as a way to take dogs back to themselves, that is, to their wilder, predomesticated selves. This is a somewhat romantic notion, and an important thing to keep in mind is that dogs enjoy exploration in the safety of their pack (that's us). As the pack leaders, we have a responsibility to approach hiking with our canine family in a way that is fun, safe, and at the same time keeping to human rules and courtesies. To that end, it is our job to make sure our dogs are responsive and trail-ready and that we are prepared to handle any emergencies that may arise, or better yet, prevent them from arising. This section offers a primer on readying yourself and your dog for fun times on Arizona's trails.

Good Dogs Require Good Owners

The importance of basic obedience training cannot be overstated. Poorly prepared dogs—and the hikers who have a casual attitude about dog trail etiquette—lend fuel to the ongoing controversies about dogs in public parks, on public lands, and in wilderness areas. Unfortunately, good trail dogs and their responsible owners pay the price by losing access to the outdoors one trail at a time.

It is as important to socialize dogs for your outdoor adventures as it is

Opposite: Crossing Rock Creek, Ken is stalled by Artemis—ever curious and enjoying the cool waters of this high-desert stream.

Didi looking at the trail behind while enjoying a water break

to physically condition them for hiking. Arizona's rampant sunshine prac-
tically demands outdoor activity for residents and tourists alike. Even
trails that are more than an hour away from our metropolitan areas can
see heavy usage on weekends in peak seasons. Many allow at least two,
if not all, of the following activities: hiking, mountain biking, horseback
riding, target shooting, and hunting. You should cultivate in your dog
an ability to interact calmly with other dogs and other people, and to
respond to your leash and voice control (with no barking) around
horses, bicycles, and shotgun or pistol fire. For many dogs, the latter is

terrifying. Only two trails in this book occur near a shooting range, but many trails are used for access to hunting areas. If your dog reacts badly to thunder or fireworks, it is a good sign that you should avoid trails during hunting season—check with the Arizona Game and Fish Department or the land management agency listed in the hike write-up for nearby hunting activity.

While there are plenty of resources available in books and online that offer tips on working with your dog privately on basic obedience skills, group classes have a real edge over that approach because the socialization aspect is built in to the setting, and your dog must learn to respond to your commands over the white noise of distraction.

The good news is that this process—essentially, learning how to communicate better with your dog and teaching her to be comfortable in a variety of settings—is also terrific fun, and very rewarding when you see the results.

Health Concerns for Your Dog

Domesticated dogs are no more inherently athletic than we domesticated humans are. It looks shocking in black and white, yet it is true. So why do we operate under the expectation that dogs can simply pick up and go hiking with us with little or no conditioning?

Building up to that pristine mountain vista is easy if you avoid "panic training." Start with one short walk each morning and night and everyday keep this up (your dog will be the best alarm clock you have ever known: just try to sleep late once your dog gets used to this routine). Add more intensive training sessions to your routine once you and your dog have worked the kinks out of muscles and joints, which will take about a month, perhaps less time for younger dogs. Try to get up to at least an hour per session, with at least four training sessions per week.

If you mix up the areas you walk with your dog, you will have not only the aerobic and muscle-building benefits that come with regular training, but you will accustom your dog's pads to a variety of surfaces, a common feature of Arizona's diverse landscapes. Luckily, urban areas throughout the state have access to flat footpaths, hilly rambles, and trails with steep mountain grades—not to mention neighborhood streets, parks, and canal rights-of-way that are becoming popular dog-walking spots.

Altogether, within two months you and your dog should be ready to field test your conditioning in less familiar, wilder settings. As with the aerobic conditioning, start out slowly on the trail and build up to longer distances and more significant elevation changes over time.

A note of caution when you are hiking in the desert lowlands or chaparral: heat stress can set in with ambient temperatures lower than 80° F, depending on the effort being expended. What that means is that you will rarely be able to do hikes of any length in the summer in the Phoenix and Tucson areas. Keep your dog's conditioning up in the summer by doing your longer sessions in the very early morning and keep your evening walks short (asphalt and concrete retain the sun's searing heat well after dark, hence the phrase, "urban heat island").

Now that this regimen is an everyday part of your life, you can pick up the leash anytime and head out for a fun seasonal hike.

Permits and Regulations

No special permits are needed for hiking with dogs. However, with very few exceptions, dogs must be on a leash no longer than 6 feet and owners are required to properly dispose of waste (see next section). Leash rules are required both as a courtesy to other trail users and for your dog's protection, and it is important that those of us who love to hike with our dogs set excellent examples on our outings: wherever leashes are required, use them. Some Bureau of Land Management and U.S. Forest Service trails allow dogs to hike under voice control once past the busier trailhead, and these are noted in hike descriptions. But even on "no-leash" trails, you should always stay alert, and keep your dog close at heel and the leash handy.

The importance of being a good ambassador for hiking with dogs cannot be overstated. Nearly all national parks ban dogs from hiking trails. The City of Phoenix is considering banning dogs from at least one popular trail, with other ban proposals expected to follow. The State of Arizona bans dogs from hiking in several state parks. Those of us who hike responsibly with our dogs—following both the rules and the demands of common courtesy, such as picking up dog waste—can do much to reverse this trend.

One last note on permits: many land management agencies require a day use or overnight pass (see hike write-ups for locations of fee stations where passes are required), and some also require a permit for long-term stays, such as backpacking trips. Contact the land management agency for the trail in question to confirm pass rates or to obtain your backcountry permit.

Go Lightly on the Land

Arizona's beautiful—and beautifully varied—landscapes beckon to travelers and residents alike. Thanks to our mild winters and rather predictable rainy seasons, Arizona's public lands are enjoyed by ever-greater numbers of hikers, birding enthusiasts, horseback riders, cyclists, climbers, and trail runners. No matter what the focus of our outdoor adventure is, it is important

Teri and Charlie after a romp in Sycamore Creek along the Parsons Spring Trail

to keep in mind that every time we enjoy a trail, we change it in some small way. Woodland and desert creatures must surely think of us as the Godzillas of the wilderness—big, clumsy mutants who lumber along with no malice but who still manage with our carelessness and enthusiasm to leave a lot of damage in our wake.

With only a jot more care and preparation, we can tame our inner Godzillas and reduce the negative impacts of our outings. This is especially important in the desert Southwest, for while these arid landscapes have tough—some might say harsh—defenses, they are very fragile ecologically. Springs have a lushness that belies their vulnerability to disturbance. Treat them as you would any pristine water source: avoid unnecessary off-trail travel in their surrounds; camp at least 200 feet away; do not let your dog dig near them; and go at least 200 feet away to void your bladder or defecate (and bury your waste and your dog's waste properly where appropriate—pack out what you cannot bury).

Practicing such simple conservation techniques as outlined by the nonprofit outdoor education group, Leave No Trace, helps you get the maximum enjoyment from hiking, camping, or backpacking with your dog, while making sure that others' enjoyment—as well as the landscape itself—is not diminished. The cornerstones of the Leave No Trace ethic are:

- Plan Ahead and Prepare
- Travel and Camp on Durable Surfaces
- Protect and Conserve Water Resources
- Pack It In, Pack It Out
- Properly Dispose of What You Can't Pack Out
- Leave What You Find
- Use Fire Responsibly
- Be Considerate of Other Visitors

For more information, go to *www.lnt.org* and as always, contact the trail's land manager for specific rules or guidelines recommended for that area.

Camp Care: Cleanup

Keeping a clean camp without soiling your environment—or attracting wildlife with your chili-surprise leftovers—requires some finesse, but it's easy to do.

After meals, if you don't want to give leftovers to your dog, scrape away all food from your pots, plates, and utensils into a bag that seals and pack it out. (Never throw out leftovers. Ever.) Rinse the dishes in plain water from your stores or if available, water from a nearby source. Collect water and move at least 200 feet away—about 75 adult steps—from the water source. Lightly soap your dishes using a dab of biodegradable cleanser, wipe them out with a towel or bandanna, then rinse. The same care to conserve water and reduce the amount of chemicals left in the landscape should be taken when washing your body.

At some time or other, we've all happened upon someone else's makeshift toilet, usually marked with undecomposed human (or canine) waste and sometimes even tattered toilet paper.

Here are some tips to help reduce the chances that a simple call of nature will spread disease (and contempt!) among your fellow trail users. It's simple: all human and dog waste—including tampons (or the like) and toilet paper—must be packed out of narrow river canyons. In forests, however, it is fine to bury feces in a cathole, though you must still pack out tampons and toilet paper. To make a cathole, dig from 6 to 8 inches down into the soil in a spot well away from camp, trail, and water sources. Refill the hole once you've deposited the waste, and then use leaf litter, sticks, or rocks to camouflage the cathole. One important note for desert hikers: desert soils have less organic material to aid in decomposition. For short trips, pack out all waste. For long desert backpacking trips, use a shallower cathole (4 to 6 inches deep) because the sun and heat will have to take over for the paucity of microorganisms. Be sure to disperse your catholes so that waste does not become concentrated in any one area.

Good Canine Trail Etiquette

Good trail dog-hiker teams are ambassadors of sorts. Even if we are not sharing wild places with other users at the same time, we share these places nonetheless. Moreover, the concept of trail etiquette includes how we interact with the trail and the land as well as other users.

It almost sounds too simple to say that courtesy—and this extends to your dog as well—is the only principle to follow. There is no devil lurking in the details here, however.

What courtesy looks like on the ground is this:

- On- or off-leash, dogs must be under control. Other trail users, friendly though they may be, do not necessarily appreciate an unfamiliar dog's excited yips, sniffs, or galloping charges as they pass.

- Rights-of-way follow a logical, well-established pattern: all users yield to equestrians and should avoid startling horses for safety's sake; uphill travelers have the right-of-way (unless they choose to take a break from their huffing and puffing while letting downhill travelers pass).
- If you are hiking with your dog in a group, the group should travel single file and to the right side of the trail. This allows smooth two-way traffic and a passing lane if faster users approach from behind you.
- Adhere to the specific trail rules for the area you are visiting.
- Use a leash when and where it is required and if common sense demands it.
- Keep your dog on a lead at night if it is not possible for her to bed down in your tent with you.
- In moister climes, you may use 6–8" catholes to bury waste as long as you are at least 200 feet away from water; in deserts, use 4-6" catholes or, ideally, pack out waste.
- See that your dog does not dig a hole to lie down in when on a rest break or bedding down for the night. Avoid fragile soils, such as cryptogammic (or cryptobiotic) crusts in the desert since they take generations to recover from disturbance; choose durable surfaces for your rest spots or campsites and your dog will be less likely to dig.
- As a general rule, it is best to lead no more than one dog per person.
- Keep a respectful distance between wildlife that you come across and you and your dog. Boost your camera and eyes with telephoto lenses and field glasses.
- If you come upon archaeological or historic sites, enjoy them but do not disturb them—others will appreciate finding the area pristine.
- When following an established trail, use it. Cutting switchbacks or blazing new trails increases erosion and damages the flora. (In some places, like city parks, it is a ticketable offense as well.) If you are visiting an area where there are no official trails, use the informal footpaths that exist rather than make new trails. If that is not possible, head for your destination in the most direct manner possible and travel on durable surfaces when you can.

A saguaro seedling along the Sutherland Trail

Myths and Misunderstandings about Dogs

While more hikers are taking their canine companions along on outdoor jaunts, some myths persist about the perceived dangers of taking dogs into the backcountry. Let's set the record straight.

Myth: Dogs Frighten Off Wildlife

Reality: Dogs who are under control—that is, dogs who remain quiet and who do not bolt, even if they are off-leash—will not by their very presence disturb wildlife. In fact, my dog's acute senses are far ahead of mine: her body language upon sighting wildlife alerts me to foraging elk beyond the edges of the meadow or to lizards scampering quietly among boulders. Still, this takes training, since for many dogs a natural instinct is to chase running or chirping wildlife. If you are lucky enough to be traveling in an area where off-leash travel is permitted and wildlife are plentiful—especially during early morning, when wildlife tend to be most active—and you have any question about your dog's ability to heel, simply put her back on the leash.

Myth: Dogs Chase Wildlife

Reality: Well-trained dogs—and responsible owners who keep their dogs under control and on-leash where it is required or makes sense—will not have such confrontations. While urban canines will probably be curious about wildlife, they are keenly aware that we are their pack and are generally going to be wary of animals they see from the trail. (There's a reason that the adage goes "curiosity killed the cat," which, incidentally, is another myth—but that's another book.) The upshot here is that badly trained apples are spoiling the so-called barrel.

Myth: Dogs Spread Disease

Reality: Actually, dogs are more at risk from disease than the cause of it. The best evidence suggests that dogs are more likely to get tick-borne diseases from wildlife than they are to infect wildlife. With regard to waterborne diseases, which all mammals carry and spread, humans are the biggest culprits. Vaccinate your dog for giardia, properly dispose of all your waste (pack it out when it is not appropriate to bury it), and always treat the water you take from springs and streams.

Myth: Dogs Damage Fragile Environments

Reality: Not by themselves, they don't. Compare the ecological (and literal) footprint of a dog's soft pad to that of a treaded hiking shoe or boot, bicycle treads, or the hooves of cattle, horses, or elk. The etiquette issue looms large: sensitive areas should be traversed on trail. When off-trail travel is permitted, responsible hikers will minimize their impacts as much as possible by traveling on existing, informal use paths or on durable surfaces. And regardless of your route, pack out all waste that cannot be buried.

Wildlife Cautions

Black bears and mountain lions are wondrous creatures to enjoy from a distance as they sun or graze in wild places. Bears like shady pine forests and chaparral, but it is not unheard of to find them at lower elevations. Mountain lions range all over Arizona, but prefer rugged river canyons, mountains, and rocky foothills. This means that a large number of Arizona's trails that traverse bear or mountain lion habitat also happen to be great places to bring dogs. Both bears and mountain lions are generally shy creatures, provided you haven't startled them or extended an invitation at mealtime.

A leashed dog and a clean camp are the best ways to prevent confrontations with bears and mountain lions. Here are some simple dos and don'ts to keep in mind when you are traveling in territories where you might encounter bears or mountain lions.

Tips to avoid bear confrontations:

- Leash your dog; keep your dog on a lead at night if she sleeps outside of your tent.
- Make noise as you hike.
- Notice if there is bear sign in an area—learn to recognize their scat (droppings), and look for claw marks on trees; this will allow you to stay alert for bears.
- Steer clear of their favorite food sources such as berry patches; in particular, don't let your dog approach dead animals: these could be bear caches.
- Do not use scented personal items; store toothpaste and such items carefully in camp.
- If you are camping, cook and eat well outside of your tent and clean your camp carefully.
- Use separate bags such as stuff sacks to store food, including dog food, and hang the bags from a tree or trunk at least 12 feet off the ground and 4 feet from the trunk.
- Do not entice wild animals closer with food.

When your best efforts fail:

- If you sight a bear, give it a wide berth or leave the area.
- Do not run. Remain calm and keep your dog under control.
- Make yourself appear larger (open your jacket above your head and hold your arms out).
- Don't look directly at the bear—in bear language, that's a challenge.
- Bears are known to make bluff charges. Don't run; you cannot outrun a bear: for their bulk, they are nimble runners. Know that black bears can climb trees, grizzly bears cannot.
- If a bear charges from close range because it was surprised, lie down and play dead. If the bear charges from a distance, fight back aggressively.
- In bear country, carry bear deterrent, a concentrated pepper spray. You must wait until the bear is in range to fire the spray, which has a range of about 20 feet.

As we humans have expanded our reach and range throughout the desert Southwest, we have started to pay more attention to our interactions with mountain lions.

As noted above, these shy creatures will generally avoid us—it's not that we're not great neighbors (though sometimes, we've proven that we aren't very neighborly), it's just that we're not on their radar.

When we do interact with mountain lions, in most cases the meetings are casual. Attacks are extremely rare. Some of the tips for avoiding confrontation—and ensuring that an unavoidable confrontation will not turn tragic--are similar to those for bears. But the differences are critical.

Tips to avoid mountain lion confrontations:
- As with bears, keep your dog leashed.
- Ideally, do not hike alone.
- Avoid dead animals—that means your dog should, too.

If you meet up with a mountain lion that is curious about you, here is what you do:
- Never run away; face the animal and do not be afraid to challenge it with eye contact.
- Try to appear large by flapping your jacket and waving your arms.
- Slowly back away while maintaining your aggressive, enlarged stance.
- Pick up children to prevent them from running, which could trigger the cat's predator response.

If the mountain lion stands its ground:
- Stay in your "stand and deliver" stance.
- Throw things at hand—but don't break eye contact or expose your back when reaching for them.
- Shout.

Chances are, the mountain lion is just being curious. When it realizes you are not worth the trouble, it typically will back off.

In the highly unlikely circumstance of a mountain lion attack, fight back

Opposite: Sentinel of the desert, still on duty

aggressively. Use your jacket, hat, walking stick, rocks, even your bare hands—all have proven successful at driving off an attacking lion.

Porcupines range throughout some northern and southeastern Arizona forests, but operate under a "live and let live" policy with dogs. Problem is, curious dogs who paw or sniff a porcupine can get a rude awakening! What's worse, if your dog reacts aggressively to pain, she can pick up hundreds of quills as she thrashes and snaps at the porcupine. The best way to avoid this situation is to make sure your dog stays under control at all times.

Skunks particularly like pinyon juniper woodlands in Arizona. If your dog startles a skunk and gets sprayed, treat her eyes first: flush with lots of warm water and as soon as you can, apply drops of warm olive oil. Time and frequent bathing of Fido's coat are the best methods to deal with the lingering eau de skunk. A bigger concern with skunks is the fact that they can carry rabies—keep your dog's shots current and as always, keep her under control!

The imposing desert and dramatic mesas of the Paria Canyon-Vermilion Cliffs Wilderness

Weather and Climate

The image most often associated with Arizona is the saguaro cactus—a symbol popularized by and forever connected with the parched landscapes of Hollywood westerns. But as arid as Arizona is, one of the keys to the lushness of our deserts and montane forests is the fact that there are two rainy seasons: December through February and July through September.

The summer monsoon season brings turbulent late afternoon squalls, complete with high winds, blowing dust (particularly near disturbed areas such as farms and new construction sites), torrential bursts of rain, flash floods, and fierce lightning. Winter rains and snowstorms tend to be gentler affairs, though they will usually be accompanied by significant lightning danger as well.

Even though Arizona's climate is dominated by sunny days and storms tend to be fairly predictable, you should always check weather conditions before setting out. While backpacking, use a National Oceanic and Atmospheric Administration—NOAA—weather radio to stay abreast of changing weather patterns. As a precaution, camp on durable surfaces in open fields away from trees, bodies of water, and large rock formations. If for any reason you find yourself in the path of a storm while you are on the trail, here are some ways to avoid lightning strikes:

- Stay away from mountaintops and ridges.
- Keep clear of bodies of water.
- If your hair stands on end or if you see your dog's hair standing on end, move immediately! Static electricity often indicates an imminent ground strike.
- If there happens to be a building nearby, get into it and keep away from windows and doors since they may conduct lightning into the interior of your shelter. Do not shelter under trees.
- If there is no shelter available, remove all metal objects from your person (remember to remove the identification and vaccination tags from your dog's collar), and crouch down on the balls of your feet, keeping your dog close, until the storm passes.

One of the most serious weather-related considerations in Arizona is the heat in our lower elevations. Temperatures have been known to soar past 120° F in the summer—and there can be a nearly 50° F difference between day and nighttime temperatures. Even in spring and autumn,

Boulder-hopping and wading through water are real doggie treats in the desert.

when temperature variance is not so dramatic, the same trail can offer a very cool early morning hike or an uncomfortably warm one by noon, so layer accordingly and always have sun protection on Arizona trails. For all hikes that are recommended in spring, summer, and autumn—this is especially true for summer—plan on going early in the day for maximum fun on the trail.

Exposure to cold and wind—especially if you are slogging through streams—can also pose hazards in Arizona, even at low elevations. Under the right (or wrong) conditions, both humans and dogs can experience hypothermia with ambient temperatures as high as 50° F. Outside the urban heat islands, temperatures can plunge after sundown in autumn, winter, and spring. If you are traveling in winter, be sure to have an extra warm layer for yourself and your dog and bring along a towel to dry your dog should she get wet.

In short, the best way to avoid cutting a trip short due to weather concerns is to heed the seasonal recommendations offered for these trails, check the weather forecast, and call the relevant agency for up-to-the-minute trail conditions.

The Essentials
Gear for You and Your Dog

Hiking truly isn't a walk in the park—even when it is. The appropriate gear is not about making a fashion statement, but about safety and ensuring an enjoyable outdoor experience for you and your dog.

One key gear system for Arizona is sun protection, regardless of your destination. A wide-brimmed, lightweight hat is a must, and will work year-round unless you are snowbound. In that instance, get a good fleece hat for warmth and don't forget to apply sunscreen. Even on mild days, protect your skin from exposure by wearing breathable, synthetic, long-sleeved shirts and field pants—not only is this sun-wise, but it really is the best way to keep cool.

Dogs need sun protection, too. Train your dog to wear a hat for exposed trails—children's sizes are just right for most dogs. If your dog has light-colored skin on her nose, apply doggy sunscreen. Don't use yours—go for the sunscreen specially formulated for a dog's pH balance, and one that won't maker her sick if she licks it off before she becomes accustomed to wearing it.

Footgear is something you should splurge on. Your primary footwear will depend on the terrain you prefer to travel on, the distances you hike, and the weight you carry in your pack. If you are average weight for your sex and carry more than a 30-pound pack (or if you have wobbly ankles), then sturdy, at least mid-height, boots with shanks, and Vibram or other shock-absorbing treads are a must. For shorter jaunts without a pack, you will get sufficient stability from a good pair of trail runners or other low-rise hiking shoe, provided the outer sole of the shoe is wider than the footbed (this adds ankle support without the bulk of a boot). For streamside jaunts, a good pair of technical sandals is helpful—some, like Chacos, have shanks in them for support. Fit is critical, so plan to spend some time with an expert bootfitter to arrive at the right boot or shoe for your needs.

Baby your feet further with good hiking socks. By "good," I mean "not cotton." Cotton retains moisture and thereby promotes blistering. Contemporary synthetic or wool-blend socks are made such that, unless you are especially prone to blistering or heading to extremely cold climates, you should never have to layer your socks again. Buy your socks when you are trying on your boots—this will take some of the guesswork out of finding your best fit and comfort preferences.

Your dog's pads need attention in the gear department, too. Sure, you will spend some time conditioning Fido to toughen her pads, but the footpaths on both desert lowlands and montane trails tend to have at least some rocky stretches. My recommendation is to fit your dog for booties, get her accustomed to wearing them on short outings, and then you will be set when and if you need them. Many brands are on the market now (see Appendix for dog gear manufacturers), but you should get booties that are loose enough on top to flex with the dog's leg and that have non-slip bottoms. As for humans, fit is key. Dogs' toes spread as they walk, and booties must be loose enough for the toes to move but not so loose that they create blisters.

Other dog gear you should have on hand include a light vest for cooler nights, or caution-colored vests for her to wear on-trail if you happen to be hiking in areas that border or overlap with hunting grounds. You should invest in collapsible bowls. They fold away to nothing, weigh little; get two so that you have one for food and one for water. For overnight trips, your dog might also like a small sleeping pad of her very own.

Wouldn't you like some help carrying all this gear? Thanks to innovative manufacturers, sturdy and practical doggy backpacks are available. Don't ask your dog to carry more than 20 percent of her body weight, though, and be sure to pack the load evenly.

The Ten Essentials

Given the choice of climates and landscapes in Arizona, you will need to vary your "to bring" list quite a bit, but there are some items that should never leave your pack (except when you need to replenish stores). I like to keep a checklist that I can refer to whenever I set out so that I am never caught without these items.

1) **Extra clothing.** Save a tiny bit of room in your pack—you won't need much!—for lightweight or featherweight underlayers (top and bottom), which work year-round whether you want to boost your sun protection or your insulation against the cold. During winter, add a lightweight fleece vest and a pair of good synthetic socks to your spare clothing stash.

2) **Extra food and water.** A good rule of thumb is to bring along one extra meal and two extra snacks in case injury or weather forces you and your dog to stay on the trail longer than planned. And, just as important, even if you are heading to an area that has a reliable water source, always bring

extra water: injury or other emergencies might keep you from getting to the next water source.

3) **Sun protection.** A wide-brimmed hat, sunglasses, and sunscreen are must-haves for any hiking in the desert Southwest.

4) **Knife or multi-tool.** A properly sheathed knife (or folding knife) is handy for short trips. If you like to camp or backpack, bring instead a multi-use tool that includes a knife, a screwdriver, and pliers: these are indispensable for repairing damaged gear.

5) **First-aid kit.** My first recommendation is for something that must be carried in your head, not your pack: a first-aid training course (see Appendix). The kit itself can be quite basic, but should at minimum include gauze, bandages, antiseptic, and pain relievers. A desert-ready first-aid kit must also include a small comb with widely spaced teeth for removing cactus joints from skin or boots. Tweezers or hemostats work well to remove thorns or individual cactus spines. Take along an emergency cache of medication you need on a daily basis, in case you get delayed.

6) **Fire starter.** Fire-starting paste, nuggets, or ribbon work to ignite even damp wood.

7) **Matches.** Waterproof/windproof matches are available and worth the minimal investment because, unlike book matches and disposable lighters, they are reliable in wet or windy weather.

8) **Flashlight.** You won't notice the weight of most modern compact flashlights in your pack, and if you end up lingering on the trail after dark you will be thankful you carried one. Remove the batteries between trips, test your flashlight before heading out, and carry an extra bulb and batteries along.

9) **Map.** Know how to use a topographical map, and always carry one for the area you are visiting.

10) **Compass.** The only drawback of a GPS system is that without batteries, they are useless—and they devour batteries quickly. Take a compass along and be sure you know how to use it.

In addition to the ten essentials, I always wrap one of my water bottles with duct tape that I can peel off as needed. I also slip an old compact disc into a small pouch for use as a signaling device; this is a good alternative to a mirror since backpacks see more abuse than baggage at an airport and why risk the bad luck? When I know I'm heading out for more than a day hike, I like to carry three lightweight, superabsorbent, and quick-drying towels: one that is tea-towel-sized for dishes and two that are 15 inches by 40 inches—one for me, and another to have on hand in case I need to dry off my dog. Finally, regardless of the length of the trip I am planning for, I like to bring a few gallon-sized, sealable plastic bags for waste that must be packed out.

The Ten Canine Essentials

Above are your essentials. For your dog you should also have the Ten Canine Essentials:

1) **Obedience training.** Before you set foot on a trail, make sure your dog is trained and can be trusted to behave appropriately when faced with other hikers, other dogs, wildlife, and an assortment of strange scents and sights in the backcountry.

2) **Doggy backpack.** Lets the dog carry its own gear.

3) **Basic first-aid kit.** (Details listed below.)

4) **Dog food and trail treats.** You should pack more food than your dog normally consumes since it will be burning more calories than normal, and if you do end up having to spend an extra night out there, you need to keep the pup fed, too. Trail treats serve the same purpose for the dog as they do for you—quick energy and a pick-me-up during a strenuous day of hiking.

5) **Water and water bowl.** Don't count on there being water along the trail for the dog. Pack enough extra water to meet all your dog's drinking needs.

6) **Leash and collar, or harness.** Even if your dog is absolutely trained to voice command and stays at heel without a leash, sometimes leashes are required by law or just by common courtesy. You should have one handy at all times.

7) **Insect repellent.** Be aware that some animals, and some people, have strong negative reactions to DEET-based repellents. So, before leaving home, dab a little DEET-based repellent on a patch of your dog's fur to see if she reacts to it. Look for signs of drowsiness, lethargy, and/or nausea. Restrict repellent applications to those places the dog can't lick—the back of the neck and around the ears (staying well clear of the eyes and inner ears) are the most logical places mosquitoes will be looking for exposed skin to bite.

8) **ID tags and picture identification.** Your dog should always wear ID tags, and I'd heartily recommend microchipping her as well. To do this, a vet injects a tiny encoded microchip under the skin between the dog's shoulders. If your dog ever gets lost and is picked up by Animal Control, or is taken to a vet's office, a quick pass over the dog's back with a hand scanner will reveal the chip, and allow the staff at that shelter or hospital to identify your dog and notify you. Microchipping is so prevalent that virtually every veterinarian and animal shelter automatically scans every unknown dog they come in contact with to check for chips. The picture identification should go in your pack. If your dog gets lost, you can use the picture to make flyers and handbills to post in the surrounding communities.

9) **Dog booties.** These can be used to protect the dog's feet from rough ground or harsh vegetation. They are also great at keeping bandages secure if the dog damages its pads.

10) **Compact roll of plastic bags and trowel.** You'll need the bags to clean up after your dog on popular trails. When conditions warrant, you can use the trowel to take care of your dog's waste. Just pretend you are a cat—dig a small hole several inches deep in the forest duff, deposit the dog waste, and fill in the hole.

Canine First Aid
Minor Aches and Muscle Strains

The best first aid for your dog starts with prevention. Your conditioning program will stave off both minor aches and more serious injuries for both you and your dog.

For those times when you overreach your training and your dog seems to be walking more slowly or stiffly after a session or hike (and the problem doesn't appear to have resulted from an injury), keep some enteric-coated aspirin on hand and administer it according to your vet's instructions: generally, the dosage is 5-10 mg per pound twice a day. Enteric is a specially buffered aspirin that dissolves in the intestines. Don't give your dog non-aspirin pain medication in a pinch, since aspirin substitutes can lead to liver damage, diarrhea, or appetite loss. The pain and inflammation should go away quickly. Some dogs may not be able to digest the enteric-coated aspirin, however, and may pass the pills in their stool. Check with your vet for other pain relief options. In the meantime, don't overlook the value of alternate application of hot and cold packs.

If this happens to your dog, ease back your training and scale down your hikes a bit for a short time and then build back up more slowly. Consider adding a glucosamine supplement to your dog's food. Glucosamine helps build stronger joints and cartilage, while reducing inflammation. Again, check with your vet about dosages.

Snakes

Native venomous snakes include the rattlesnake—seventeen species—and the diminutive coral snake. Rattlesnakes occur almost everywhere in Arizona; coral snakes also range widely (mainly in central and southern Arizona) but are almost never seen. Many nonvenomous snakes make their homes in Arizona's wild places as well. Having said this, you should know that snakebite is quite rare. It can be serious, however.

In keeping with the theme of prevention, many vets and wildlife managers in Arizona recommend some form of snake aversion training. (See Appendix for contacts through the Red Cross, Humane Society, and parks departments that conduct some combination of wilderness preparation, snakebite prevention, and first-aid classes.)

Now, your obedience training and expert on- and off-leash control will go a long way toward preventing snake bites—as will exercising common sense and not letting your dog put her nose or paws where you cannot see what might meet them. Step on rocks and logs rather than over them; your dog will follow. Warm spring afternoons and early summer evenings in all rocky, outcroppy areas throughout the state show some species of rattlesnake active and in residence.

Fortunately, dogs aren't nearly as susceptible to rattlesnake venom as people are. Still, you will need to treat the wound, and most outlying veterinary clinics have access to antivenom (generally, the inner-city vets will not). You should check with your own vet while planning your hike to find out what to do in the worst case.

Immediate first aid is simple—the best snakebite first-aid device is actually your car key. In other words, pick up and carry your dog if possible and get her to a professional for treatment. Do not ice the wound: ice can speed necrosis or tissue damage around the wound, as well as complicate the vet's assessment of the seriousness of the bite and treatment to be followed. Keep the wound lower than the heart to slow circulation of the venom. It is no longer recommended to apply a tourniquet, cut, or suck the wound. In short, stay calm but get your dog to a vet as soon as possible.

It is worthwhile to quickly check the wound to at least confirm that what has bitten your dog is a venomous snake. Nonpoisonous snakes like king snakes or bull snakes will strike and leave many small puncture wounds in a crescent shape, whereas a rattler will leave two to four deep puncture marks. You must still seek treatment for nonvenomous snakebites, since secondary infections can arise and your dog may need antibiotics.

Other Venomous Critters

Some toads in Arizona can poison a dog with a secretion from their paratoid glands. The symptoms include drooling, seizures, rapid heartbeat, rapid breathing, and loss of consciousness. Keeping your dog under control—especially near permanent waterways—will prevent accidental poisoning and a panicked trip back to your vet. If your dog mouths or nuzzles a toad and then exhibits these symptoms, flush her mouth and eyes with cool water and seek veterinary care right away.

The tiny bark scorpion has a big bite when it comes to venom. If your dog gets stung, you may treat the wound with ice before seeking treatment—tissue necrosis will not set in as it does with rattlesnake strikes.

Flora to Watch Out for

Poison ivy is more common in Arizona than either poison sumac or poison oak. Poison ivy occurs mostly in moister areas such as along the banks of waterways. These plants will not irritate or blister canine skin, but your dog's coat can transfer the plant's oils to your skin. Just be sure to wash your dog carefully if you see that she has come into contact with any of these plants. If there's no water available give your dog a vigorous dust bath—use your bandanna to work the dust through her coat so that you don't transfer any of the oils to your skin.

Ferns, horse nettles, nightshade, and mistletoe all contain enough toxins to make dogs sick to their stomachs; be sure that your dog doesn't ingest any. Most dogs won't be interested in nibbling on ferns, but in a land of little green, ferns can provide temptation!

Foxtails are a much more serious threat, because these cunning seeds can lodge deep in your dog's skin. The areas most at risk are the tender spots between your dog's toes, her eyes, her nose, her throat, and her ears. Foxtails contain reversed barbs, which causes them to burrow in one direction and makes them very difficult to remove. They are painful and can lead to infections, so if you are unsuccessful at removing them, seek treatment.

Getting ready to set out on a desert adventure

Cacti pose less of a first-aid challenge than you might think, unless your dog is out of control and bounds into many pads or joints. A comb is useful to remove spines still attached to the plant—just be sure to grasp the comb and aim to dislodge the cactus away from you and your dog's body. You will need to use tweezers or hemostats to remove individual spines. If a piece of spine gets lodged under the skin, chances are it will work its way out; but watch the wound and if it does not appear to be healing, seek treatment. Though cactus spines lodged in your dog's mouth can be painful, they often dissolve. Again, keep an eye on such injuries and call your vet if you are unsure about the appropriate time to bring your dog in.

Dehydration and Heat Stress

In hot, arid climates, dehydration and heat stress are serious risks. Your conditioning routine will help to acclimate your dog, and heeding the season recommendations for the hikes included in this trail guide will also prevent serious heat-related stress and injury.

Dogs with small noses and mouths like pugs, bulldogs, and boxers, who simply can't get enough air over their tongues to cool off, are especially sensitive to the heat. But regardless of breed, take lots of water breaks with your dog and always bring more than you think you need. Dogs need at least an ounce per pound per day without exertion on a mild day. Keep in mind that heat stress can set in with temperatures below 80° F, depending on the amount of exposure on trail and the level of exertion. If your dog is experiencing one type of heat stress, heat exhaustion, she will pant incessantly, seek shade, and plop down at every opportunity. The treatment? Pay attention to her signals: let her rest and let her drink as much water as she'd like.

Dehydration is harder to discern, takes a lot longer to set in than heat exhaustion, but it is also quite serious. If your dog isn't drooling or urinating (twice an hour is about normal), if her gums are tacky and her skin doesn't retract when you pull it slightly away from the muscle, she is about 5 percent dehydrated. Let her drink more and get out of the sun and heat right away.

Heat stroke is extremely serious and exhibits similar but more extreme symptoms than heat exhaustion, such as frantic panting, difficulty breathing, vomiting, seizures, and eventually coma. A dog's normal temperature range is up to 102° F (rectal reading). In heat stroke, dogs exhibit temperatures of 105 to 111° F; their gums and ears get very red. To address this in the field, cool her head down as much as possible: shade her if you are in an exposed area, wet her down if a water source is nearby, fan her off, and help her drink if she needs assistance. Once you have stabilized your dog, go for help.

Cuts and Scrapes

Pad injuries are painful but can be treated easily in the field. Wash the affected toe or pad and apply an antiseptic ointment and bandage. You should always apply a bandage at the bottom of the foot and work your way up so as to not cut off circulation. A sock works well as a bandage in a pinch, and you can tape it onto your dog's fur. You can also close a pad wound with a liquid bandage (surgical glue or a drop of superglue also works well) once the area is cleaned. Your dog's booties will keep the bandage clean and in place as you both resume walking.

If your dog breaks a toenail, trim it if necessary and then stop the bleeding with a styptic pen if pressure alone doesn't work. Campfire ash or corn meal can work as a styptic in a pinch.

The superglue comes in handy again if your dog receives a gash from barbed wire or thorny plants like crucifixion thorn or ocotillo. Clean the cut, dry it, and superglue the area shut—this is more effective at aiding healing than is field stitching.

For a puncture, simply wash the wound and leave it open. (Be sure no thorns are lodged in the wound—use tweezers to retrieve thorns.)

Leghold Trap Extraction

In 1994, Arizona passed a forward-thinking ban on leghold traps on public lands, however, there are several circumstances under which they can still be used, including research, wildlife relocation, and rodent control. Because the scent used as bait can attract dogs, you should check with the land manager or the Arizona Game and Fish Department about whether these traps will be in use near a trail you're planning to visit. If

A lush, mixed-conifer and aspen forest swaddles an ephemeral lake at the heart of this dormant cinder cone near the San Francisco Peaks.

that is the case, follow the leash rules and keep your dog under control to avoid her getting caught.

If Fido does happen to step into a trap, remain calm, muzzle her, and talk quietly to her to calm her down. It can be very painful for your dog to be trapped, but she can do a lot more damage to her leg by panicking. When you've calmed her down, here's how you extract her: simply place one of your feet on each of the springs beside the trap's hinge. This will free the jaws—and your dog. Check that there are no broken bones, sprains, or flesh wounds that need treatment.

Doggy First-Aid Kit

Instruments:
- Scissors/bandage scissors
- Toenail clippers
- Rectal thermometer (Note: A healthy dog should show a temperature of 101° F when taken rectally)

Cleansers and disinfectants:
- 3% hydrogen peroxide
- Betadine
- Canine eyewash (available at any large, pet supply store)

Topical antibiotics and ointments (nonprescription):
- Calamine lotion
- Triple antibiotic ointment (Bacitracin, Neomycin, or Polymyxin)
- Baking soda (for bee stings)
- Vaseline
- Styptic powder

Medications:
- Enteric-coated or buffered aspirin
- Imodium-AD
- Pepto-Bismol or other antacid

Dressings and bandages:
- Gauze pads (4 inches square)
- Gauze roll
- Nonstick pads
- Adhesive tape (1-inch and 2-inch rolls)

Miscellaneous:
- Tweezers
- Muzzle or spare bandanna
- Dog boots
- Any prescription medication your dog needs

Water

It is one of life's ironies that on our travels to wild places, we must concern ourselves with water quality. The truth is, no corner of Arizona is so remote that humans, cattle, or other hosts for giardia and *E. coli* have not been there before you. If you are day hiking, it is easy enough to pack in the water you and your dog will need. If you are planning a longer trip to a location that has a reliable water source—the latest "mountain spring water" ad campaign aside—you must treat that water before drinking.

One way to do that is to boil the water. This takes time, a stove, and fuel, and you may be hampered by fire or stove restrictions. Outdoor retailers carry a range of pumps that treat water; while all of them operate as filters, not all of them will kill viruses. The old standby still works: chemical treatment with iodine or the similarly effective (and more palatable) chemical tablets now available. Be sure to follow the dosage carefully and wait the appropriate amount of time before drinking chemically treated water to ensure that the water is pure.

You may already know how difficult it can be to prevent your dog from drinking directly from a stream. One way to keep Fido drinking your painstakingly treated water supply instead is to break out her bowl frequently; slaking her thirst this way reduces her attraction to natural sources and exposure to microorganisms that can make her sick. Since this method is not 100 percent effective, talk to your vet about a giardia vaccine.

Using this Book

Trail guides are subjective snapshots of places at a moment in time. Even the most objective information provided is mutable: rivers change course, signs are removed or destroyed, trailheads are relocated, day-use fees are changed or newly imposed, and so on. Always check with the appropriate land management agency for current trail conditions and planning details. Each of the hikes in this book lists a phone number contact for the managing agency office.

You will notice that my season recommendations for exposed or desert trails are more conservative than those listed for the same trails, for example, on the U.S. Forest Service websites. When planning outings with our dogs, we have to take into account that their bodies handle the heat differently than ours do, and that they cannot clearly communicate physical distress until problems are quite serious. While your dog's breed may give you some latitude, follow the season recommendations and start with short hikes—until you are confident of your dog's conditioning.

Each hike description also includes total round-trip mileage; total hike time; hike difficulty; elevation change and high point; USGS or other reference maps; and any special notes on trail conditions.

Several factors were taken into account when assessing the difficulty ratings for hikes, namely, elevation change, exposure, terrain, and distance. You will see that some very short hikes are rated as "easy–moderate" because they contain steep sections with some rocky patches on the footpaths; conversely, a hike with easy terrain that happens to be very long often merits an "easy–moderate" rating as well. Naturally, conditioning affects your own experience on trail as much as any of these factors; you may find that a hike rated as "moderate" is a piece of cake (effort-wise), or that you and your dog have to work up to a hike rated as "easy." No matter—remember, this is not a test! These ratings are included to give you a general idea about what to expect, and the write-ups themselves offer even more specific information about the experience you and your dog are in for. My hope is that you and Fido will have fun trekking on Arizona's wild side, and that these ratings will give you the best idea of where to start, given your preparation.

How the Trails Were Selected

Simply put, these trails have been enjoyable to me and to my dogs. But what is it dogs enjoy? They like to be with their pack, certainly, they like interesting smells, they like to cover new ground, they need to be able to stay relatively cool, and they love playtime. What we like is just as simple: safe, outdoor fun in a scenic setting with physical challenge and the chance to find some solitude in nature.

In short, I selected these places for their balance of several components. All of these hikes, including those in more urban settings, offer high scenic value and at least enough shade so that you can take a cool break with your dog. Some trails offer access to water all the time—a rarity in the desert Southwest—while many more trails have access to water after rains or during spring snowmelt. Those that are bone dry all year are typically short, fun outings that you can take advantage of on milder days in the appropriate season. I avoided the most crowded trails in both our urban parks and on our federal public lands. Because some of Arizona's popular trails, however, make great outings with dogs, I sought out trails where hiking was the only use, both to increase the possibility of finding solitude and to reduce possible conflict between dogs and horses or mountain bikes. Yet I also included some multiuse trails—or trails with multiuse segments—that have low traffic from horseback riders or cyclists. I have focused on day hikes rather than overnight backpacks, though a few of those are included as well.

Trails in this book cover a wide range of Arizona's wild places: Sonoran Desert, chapparal, quiet rivulets and springs, montane forests, and alpine meadows. All of them have unique appeals and challenges. I have always enjoyed getting to know a new place in a day hike setting and then returning for a longer trip once I know what kind of experience to expect on the ground.

A brief note about several trails that I could not include in this trail guide. For now, the Barnhardt, Half Moon, and Rock Creek Trails are closed due to significant damage from the 2004 Willow Fire. This Mazatzal Wilderness trail system offered a terrific backpacking loop for you and your dog: beautifully varied and rugged landscapes with good surface paths; excellent three-season hiking from autumn through spring; autumn color; seasonal water—and spectacular waterfalls; scenic views stretching north to the Mogollon Rim; and shade from the pinyon-juniper, riparian, and ponderosa pine woodlands along your route. Only time will heal the tree canopies in this area. Forest Service personnel estimate that it may take five years (possibly longer) to rehabilitate the footpaths themselves, which experienced severe erosion damage along a number of slopes and ridges. I am confident these trails will one day find their way back into the hearts—and trip plans—of dog-hiker teams who want to explore Arizona's wild places.

With Arizona's rugged topography, it is rare to find a trail that has no steep or rocky sections whatsoever, so you will find at least some elevation change and some challenging surfaces to contend with on many of the trails in this guide. A well-conditioned dog will have no problems with these areas, and having along the appropriate gear, such as dog booties, will keep your dog padding happily in the rough stretches.

Similarly, Arizona's landscapes are a haven for rattlesnakes, and it is impossible to avoid areas where snakes like to be if you enjoy hiking year-round. As mentioned above, snake aversion training is one option. The write-ups also include specific notes on trails where you should be particularly cautious about snakes. Naturally, you should plan to stay alert in all desert and riparian areas. Following the leash rules, heeding the seasonal suggestion, and avoiding warm afternoons on spring days will significantly reduce the chances of a lethal encounter with our reptilian friends.

One thing that adds to the hiking fun is to see your dog running and playing freely. Given the strict leash rules on nearly all trails in Arizona, this does not happen as often as any of us would like. But I include a number of trails where it is possible to allow your dog—as long as she responds unfailingly to voice control—to travel without her leash away from the trailheads.

This guide offers an excellent opportunity to start hiking with your dog or to explore more of Arizona with your dog than you might have imagined you could. My hope is that you and your dog enjoy these places as much as I and my canine family have, and that using this book will help you determine how to select other dog-suitable places to hike, camp, or backpack from the hundreds of other trails available in Arizona.

Enjoy the Trails: Get Involved

None of the trails listed in this guide would be here today if outdoor enthusiasts had not turned their interest into thoughtful action to protect wild places and urban open spaces for future generations to enjoy. As blessed as Arizona is with vast stretches of public lands, pressures from development (which especially affects river systems, thanks to thirsty, ever-growing desert cities) and extractive industries (such as logging, grazing, and mining) make public lands protection and new wilderness designation an uphill battle.

As surely as though a torch has been passed, it is up to us to make sure that the places we love to hike with our two- and our four-legged companions continue to be protected and, dare we hope, expanded. Fortunately, small acts, like a well-timed phone call to a Congressperson's office, can often make a difference. Use the resources below to find out how you can affect the future of a place where you particularly love to hike:

Grand Canyon Chapter of the Sierra Club
202 E. McDowell Road, Suite 277
Phoenix, AZ 85004
602-253-8633
www.arizona.sierraclub.org

Sky Island Alliance
P.O. Box 41165
Tucson, AZ 85717-1165
520-624-7080
www.skyislandalliance.org

Canine Hiking Club of Arizona
P.O. Box 31472
Phoenix, AZ 85046
www.mydogateaz/k9hike

Arizona Wilderness Coalition
P.O. Box 529
Alpine, AZ 85920
928-339-4426
www.azwild.org

A Note About Safety

Safety is an important concern in all outdoor activities. No guide-book can alert you to every hazard or anticipate the limitations of every reader. Therefore, the descriptions of roads, trails, routes, and natural features in this book are not representations that a particular place or excursion will be safe for your party. When you follow any of the routes described in this book, you assume responsibility for your own safety. Under normal conditions, such excursions require the usual attention to traffic, road and trail conditions, weather, terrain, the capabilities of your party, and other factors. Because many of the lands in this book are subject to development and/or change of ownership, conditions may have changed since this book was written that make your use of some of these routes unwise. Always check for current conditions, obey posted private property signs, and avoid confrontations with property owners or managers. Keeping informed on current conditions and exercising common sense are the keys to a safe, enjoyable outing.

The Mountaineers Books

Northern Arizona

GRAND CANYON COUNTRY

1. Rainbow Rim to North Timp Point

Round trip: 6.5 miles
Hiking time: 3 hours
Difficulty: easy
High point: 7673 feet
Elevation gain: 160 feet
Best: April through November
Map: Timp Point USGS
Contact: Kaibab National Forest, North Kaibab Ranger Station, (928) 643-7395; or Jacob Lake Visitor Center, (928) 643-8167.

Getting there: From Flagstaff, take US Hwy 89 north through the Painted Desert, Marble Canyon, and the Vermilion Cliffs; continue on State Hwy 89A to Jacob Lake (150 miles). Here your route heads south on State Hwy 67 (you will see the Kaibab Plateau Visitor Center at this intersection); proceed 26.5 miles. Turn right onto Forest Development Road 22 and take it 10.5 miles to the junction with FDR 206. Turn left here and proceed approximately 4.5 miles to FDR 271, which you take all the way to the

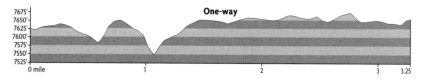

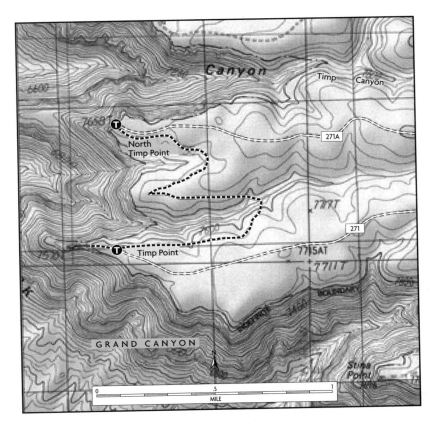

trailhead (8 miles). Park next to the corral-style fence. After your dog has had a drink and you have packed plenty of drinking water for the trail, you are ready to head out.

The scenic drive to the North Kaibab National Forest is but a teaser for this breathtaking Grand Canyon trail. Because Grand Canyon National Park does not allow dogs on its trails, many hikers have opted to make their trip to one of the world's seven wonders without their canine family members—or have foregone such an outing altogether. If you are a hiker whose heart has been broken by either of these solutions, this easy north rim trail is for you.

   Rainbow Rim Trail No. 10 rolls along five jutting fingers of the Grand Canyon's north rim for 18 miles. Layers of history—on a geologic, not human, scale—are exposed in bands of sandstone, limestone, shale, and

schist. As John Muir wrote in *The Atlantic Monthly* a century ago: "No matter how far you have wandered, or how many famous gorges and valleys you have seen, the Grand Cañon of the Colorado will seem as novel to you, as unearthly in the color and grandeur and quantity of its architecture, as if you had found it after death, on some other star. Instead of being filled with air, the vast space between the walls is crowded with Nature's grandest buildings—a sublime city of them, painted in every color, and adorned with richly fretted cornice and battlement spire in endless variety. . . . "

The North Kaibab National Forest near the canyon receives only a fraction of the visitation that the national park does, so it retains a feeling of wildness that you could not experience at the south rim of the Grand Canyon. It is possible to meet mule deer, pronghorn antelope, or even rattlesnakes along your way. If your trail dog responds unfailingly to voice control, you can let her off her leash, but keep it handy in case you do meet wildlife—or other trail users, since horses are allowed here and cycling is an increasingly popular activity on this trail.

Your hike starts from the southernmost finger, Timp Point, and ends 3 miles away at North Timp Point. From the corral, head northwest initially to a fork. To the left is a spur trail to an overlook—it is worth the trip. The trail is more exposed here but still intermittently shaded, since Timp Point is crowded with transition-zone vegetation—in addition to lofty ponderosa pines, junipers, and oaks, you brush past manzanitas, cacti, tall grasses, and wildflowers (in spring and summer). Your footpath is loose and rocky, but fairly level, and you arrive at the fingertip in 0.25 mile—exercise extreme caution on this unfenced ledge, and keep your dog close while you enjoy the scenery. To your left, a smooth, green blanket of vegetation covers the reddish layers of rock. To your right and ahead, you are peering into a long expanse of time; bare canyon walls yawn—whether they are Technicolor or pastel depends on the light—a dizzying effect while on this talon-like outcrop.

When you are ready to hit the trail proper, walk back to the fork and head left. Soon you are heading east. The occasional, ephemeral wash puts some boulders in your path, but otherwise, this is a comfortable, well-maintained, and mostly level footpath that weaves in and out of the cool shade of a beautiful forest. You turn west and brush up against

Opposite: Along the Rainbow Rim Trail from the Timp Point overlook: a rare dog's eye view of the Grand Canyon

the rim again before traveling east and then west again on the last stretch before the North Timp terminus (3.5 miles, including your detour to the overlook). Take your field glasses out and survey the canyon: far below you, feeding a thirsty band of green, the Thunder River pours from the limestone band in the Tapeats Amphitheater's north wall. Thunder River is reputed to be the shortest river in the world, as well as being the only river that is a tributary of a creek (the Tapeats). When you are ready, return the way you came. The shifting light rewards you with a unique perspective on your way back, calling to mind the adage that you cannot cross the same river twice.

It is possible to hike the Rainbow Rim's entire 36 miles round trip with just two overnight stays, or you and your dog can camp a single night on a one-way hike with a shuttle at the end of FDR 271A. Camping is allowed along the entire route (no permits necessary), and plenty of established sites exist at or near each trailhead. It is worth taking the time and effort to cache water at one or two of the trailheads, in addition to carrying more water than you think you need, to ensure that you and your dog remain well hydrated on this arid and often exposed trail.

2. Lookout Canyon Trail 120

Round trip: 24 to 32 miles
Hiking time: 2 to 3 days
Difficulty: easy–moderate
High point: 8287 feet
Elevation change: 1108 feet
Best: April through November
Maps: Big Springs, Timp Point, and De Motte Park USGS
Contact: Kaibab National Forest, North Kaibab Ranger District, (928) 643-7395; or Jacob Lake Visitor Center, (928) 643-8167

Getting there: From Flagstaff, take US Hwy 89 north through the Painted Desert, Marble Canyon, and the Vermilion Cliffs; continue on State Hwy 89A to Jacob Lake (150 miles). Here your route turns south onto State Hwy 67 (you will see the Kaibab Plateau Visitor Center at this intersection); proceed 0.3 miles to Forest Development Road 461. Turn right onto FDR 461 and continue 6 miles to FDR 462, which you take west for 3 miles to FDR 22, where you turn left. Continue 7 miles

on FDR 22 to FDR 429 and take a left. In about 0.25 mile, you come to the junction with FDR 226, where you turn right and park off-road at the sign.

Forest Development Road 226 is your trail through Lookout Canyon. The wide, graveled route runs south-southeast along a gentle uphill grade on the canyon floor. The terminus is 12 miles away, at a junction with FDR 22. It is open to hiking, cycling, horseback riding, and vehicles (typically only an issue during autumn hunting season); provided you keep the leash handy and your dog responds to voice control, you can let her enjoy some off-leash walking here.

Though you and your dog begin the hike in a broad meadow, Lookout Canyon is a limestone cleft chock full of enormous blue spruces, Engelmann spruces, white firs, ponderosa pines, and pinyon pines. Thickets of Gambel oaks and aspens provide a shock of fall color after the first frost.

Reliable water sources are a rare thing on the Kaibab Plateau, as in all of the Southwest. There are numerous ephemeral washes and springs where you may find water during snowmelt or after summer rains. The

A screen of aspens imposes on a meadow flanking the Lookout Canyon Trail.

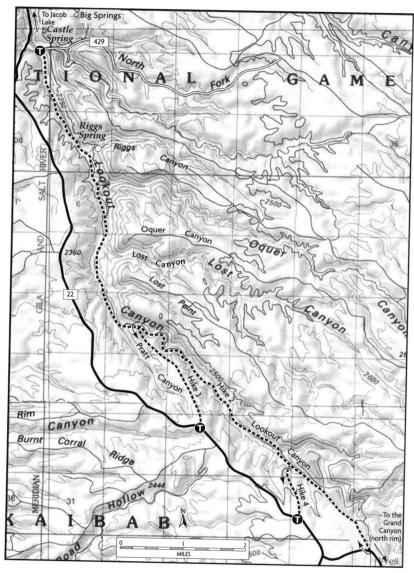

first spring—Castle Spring—is located north of FDR 429 at its intersection with FDR 226, just across from your trailhead. The second is Riggs Spring, which is tucked about 0.3 mile east (and 250 feet uphill) of the trail at the 1.6-mile mark. As always, treat any water you find from these sources and pack in extra water in case the washes and springs are dry.

You are nestled among trees within 0.4 mile of setting out. The path leads southeast initially, then makes a wide turn toward the south as the canyon walls close in. Along your way to the junction with Lookout Canyon Trail 121 and Pratt Canyon, you pass Riggs Canyon, Oquer Canyon (2.1 miles), and Lost Canyon (3 miles)—all offer good break or camping spots. The junction with Lookout Canyon Trail 122 is at 10 miles. These trail junctions heading west, though unsigned, are obvious.

You can enjoy Lookout Canyon Trail 120 as a single overnight backpack, which is 24 miles round trip if you do the entire route to FDR 22, or you can add Lookout Canyon Trails 121 and 122 for a more interesting, two-night excursion. It is very easy to cache water at the trailheads for 121 and 122 (see Hikes 3 and 4 for route and trailhead details), and you should do so to ensure that you and your dog have enough water on these typically dry trails.

3. Lookout Canyon Trail 121

Round trip: 5 miles
Hiking time: 2 hours
Difficulty: easy
High point: 8110 feet
Elevation change: 571 feet
Best: April through November
Maps: Big Springs, Timp Point, and DeMotte Park USGS
Contact: Kaibab National Forest, North Kaibab Ranger Station, (928) 643-7395; or Jacob Lake Visitor Center, (928) 643-8167

Getting there: From Flagstaff, take US Hwy 89 north through the Painted Desert, Marble Canyon, and the Vermilion Cliffs; continue on State Hwy 89A to Jacob Lake (150 miles). Here your route turns south onto State Hwy 67 (you will see the Kaibab Plateau Visitor Center at this intersection); proceed 0.3 miles to Forest Development Road 461. Turn right

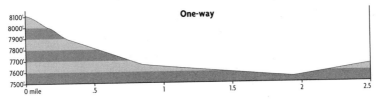

onto FDR 461 and continue for 6 miles to FDR 462, where you take another right (west). In 3 miles, take a left onto FDR 22. Just before the 8-mile mark on FDR 22, find a generic trail sign and an unmarked forest road to your left. Take that left to follow the road through a sharp right turn, then drive into the turnaround, where there is a corral-style trailhead. Park here.

The lofty branches of towering pines and aspens admit a fair amount of sunlight onto this remote trail from Pratt Canyon to Lookout Canyon. Once you have watered your dog and packed in some water for the trail, head northwest through the fence opening and onto the path. Provided your dog responds to voice control, you can let her walk off-leash here; the trail is open to cycling and horseback riding, so keep the leash handy as a courtesy to other trail users.

Your path is an old jeep road with a gravel surface that gives way occasionally to compacted forest floor. The trail leads directly northwest—with the odd twist or turn that is corrected quickly—all the way through your drop down to the junction with Lookout Canyon Trail 120 (see Hike

Sunny, tail-wagging meadows give way to cool, tail-wagging shade on your way from Pratt Canyon to Lookout Canyon.

2). The terrain is fairly flat until the final 0.3 mile. All of this adds up to a pleasant and cool forest hike with your dog.

At about 0.7 mile, take a right at the fork (markers guide you). Within another 0.2 mile, you begin to see tall cliffs to your right, their mottled beige- and charcoal-tinged walls a muted backdrop for the ponderosa pine, mixed fir, and spruce trees lining the canyon's eastern face. The terrain begins a gentle roll at about 1.5 miles. Soon the grasses and wildflowers start to swallow the path—keep your northwesterly heading and follow the trail markers to stay on track. In the spring, butterflies and moths dart drunkenly from flower to flower. You have your choice of shady, level spots to take a water break when you and your dog are ready.

A sharp left turn leads you southward briefly at 1.9 miles, where you begin a series of long switchbacks into Lookout Canyon. The gently declining trail is even more overgrown here, but between the trail markers and the erosion bumpers, you cannot miss the footpath. You bottom out at 2.3 miles and onto an unsigned road, which is the Lookout Canyon Trail 120 (FDR 226). Now that you are at ground level, the Gulliver-sized trees here are a breathtaking sight. This is your turnaround point, but you can explore in either direction for miles (or see Hike 2 for suggestions on a Lookout Canyon backpacking loop). When you and your dog are ready to head back, scale the hill and return the way you came.

4. Lookout Canyon Trail 122

Round trip: 3 miles
Hiking time: 2 hours
High point: 8319 feet
Difficulty: easy
Elevation change: 362 feet
Best: April through November
Maps: Big Springs, Timp Point, and DeMotte Park USGS
Contact: Kaibab National Forest, North Kaibab Ranger Station, (928) 643-7395; or Jacob Lake Visitor Center, (928) 643-8167

Getting there: From Flagstaff, take US Hwy 89 north through the Painted Desert, Marble Canyon, and the Vermilion Cliffs; continue on State Hwy 89A to Jacob Lake (150 miles). Here your route turns south onto State Hwy 67 (you will see the Kaibab Plateau Visitor Center at

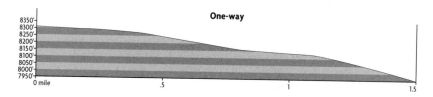

this intersection); proceed 0.3 miles to Forest Development Road 461. Turn right onto FDR 461 and continue for 6 miles to FDR 462, where you take another right (west). In 3 miles, take a left onto FDR 22. Continue 10.5 miles on FDR 22; you will see a generic trail sign here and an unmarked forest road to your left. Take that left, drive into the corral-style trailhead, and park for Lookout Canyon Trail 122.

This last and shortest trail into Lookout Canyon first leads you through an opening in a thick curtain of young aspens, a breathtaking sight after the first frost, when the aspen leaves shift from bottle green to a honeyed gold. As with Lookout Canyon Trail 121, there is no leash requirement as long as your dog responds unfailingly to voice control. Keep the leash handy as a courtesy to other trail users, should you come across any.

Your path turns northwest in 0.1 mile and continues winding around that orientation for some time. Though this trail bed was also historically a road, it is much more overgrown here and very nice under boot and paw. You and your dog are walking a gentle decline under the open canopy of mature pines, stately spruces, and at least three distinct generations of aspens. (On your return trip, there is no shortage of level places for a shady water and play break.)

The trail fades at 0.75 mile, but if you keep your northward heading, you will pick up the path. At 1 mile, you wind north-northeast and begin making a more rapid descent, veering left as you head downhill. The trail bed has a short loose, rocky patch as it winds through a quick left and then jogs northwest again. Take a sharp right (northeast) turn at 1.2 miles. You are on a long switchback, and at 1.4 miles you turn southeast. From here, you can now see the canyon floor and FDR 226 (Lookout Canyon Trail 120—see Hike 2). Some ferns greet you as you and your dog explore along the trail at the bottom of the hill; make sure Fido does not nibble their fronds.

Opposite: Towering pines and aspen groves crowd the meadows of Lookout Canyon Trail 122.

Explore this area if you like; and when you and your dog are ready, head back the way you came.

5. Sun Valley

Round trip: 2.4 miles
Hiking time: 1.5 hours
Difficulty: easy
High point: 4794 feet
Elevation change: 461 feet
Best: October through April
Map: Emmett Wash USGS
Contact: Bureau of Land Management, Arizona Strip Field Office,
  (435) 688-3230

Getting there: The trailhead for this accessible patch of starkly beautiful wilderness is located 110 miles north of Flagstaff, just off of US Hwy 89A north, approximately 3 miles west of Soap Creek and the Cliff Dwellers Lodge in Marble Canyon. A BLM wilderness sign on the west (right) marks the correct turnoff, though there is no trailhead marking as such. Park at the fence and proceed with your dog—leashes are optional if your dog responds to voice control—through the Z-gate, about 30 feet to your left. Pack in water, since none is available along this route and the trail can be intensely hot.

From the start of the hike, you are looking into sheer majesty: a vast western skyscape meets the earth along the blushing forehead of the Vermilion Cliffs. Your amble toward these tiered sandstone and shale bluffs follows an old mining road generally northwest up a ridge. The road is left over from an abandoned uranium mine. The mine was mercifully unsuccessful, ensuring that these lands could be recovered and enjoyed by future generations, and by wildlife, in a nearly pristine state.

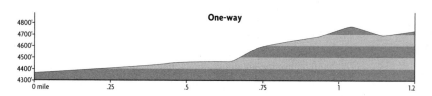

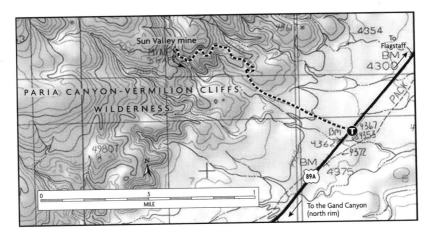

This hike to the Sun Valley mine is a good introduction to the geologically unique formations of the Paria Plateau. Along this stretch of US 89A, there are six Z-gates through which you can access the Paria Canyon–Vermilion Cliffs Wilderness with your dog (dogs are not allowed in the Paria Canyon portion of the wilderness area). Not all of them have roads or official trails, but in the appropriate seasons these are beautiful areas to explore with your dog, as long as you have your cactus comb, dog booties, sun protection, and lots of water.

The Sun Valley Trail is composed of compacted red dirt made of chinle shale: a soil that is often mucky after rains—but comfortable under boot and paw when dry. Soft sandstone boulders and outcroppings along your way sport erosion lines that resemble topographical maps. All around you is a wide desert, full of sages and cacti; rattlesnakes call this place home, too, so keep your dog close (on trail), so that she does not chance upon spines or fangs. On your way in, break out your field glasses to survey the cliffs and feast your eyes on the raptor sign. This wilderness is home to nearly two dozen species of raptors, most notably the successfully reintroduced California condors. Condors fly as high as 15,000 feet, so spotting them is a rare treat.

To the southwest (left), there is a dramatic wash that wends and slices its way through the desert. Nearly halfway to the cliffs, the road lifts you from the desert floor (0.4 mile), and you can see down into the wash's crumbly and shrubby expanses. You and your dog continue uphill, making a hairpin curve at 0.6 mile. You are now looking southeast, across Marble Canyon and into the lazily shifting pastels of Echo Cliffs and the

Painted Desert. You switch uphill on a moderate grade back to the north-west, facing the Vermilion Cliffs again, in extreme close-up. The road dips and turns west on the last stretch as you approach the old mine shaft at 1.2 miles. The opening is covered, but the weathered wood is not sturdy, so be cautious and keep your dog well away from the shaft. When you are ready for shade, head out the way you came.

Pretty, weathered outcroppings—close enough for your pooch to sniff—line the Sun Valley Trail.

FLAGSTAFF AND SURROUNDS

6. Rio de Flag South

Round trip: 2.4 miles
Hiking time: 1.5 hours
Difficulty: easy
High point: 6874 feet
Elevation change: 70 feet
Best: March through November
Map: Flagstaff West USGS
Contact: City of Flagstaff Parks and Recreation Department,
(928) 779-7690

Getting there: In Flagstaff, from Route 66, head south on Beaver Street near the Northern Arizona University campus, then east on Butler Avenue. Turn right (south) onto Lone Tree; when you come to Brannen Circle, take a left, then take another immediate left into the parking area.

Your trailhead is just over the hill from the parking area, to the north. You will see a Flagstaff Urban Trail sign, as well as a Mutt Mitt dispenser

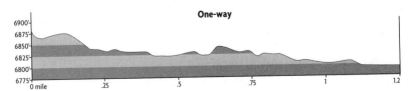

One-way

(convenient if you have forgotten to bring your own bags to clean up after your dog). Once your dog is watered—pack water in for the trail—and leashed, you will turn right, or east, to follow your trail.

The Rio de Flag South Trail, like the Buffalo Park Loop (Hike 7), offers Flagstaff residents and visitors an opportunity for a highly scenic, conditioning hike. An added benefit of Rio de Flag, especially after spring snowmelt and summer rains, is that it also gives your dog a chance to enjoy some splash time, though at the upper end of the trail only. It also feels more remote, thanks to the high canyon walls and screen of trees; deer are still spotted here, and many wildlife flock to the reclaimed water plant and wetland at the trail's terminus. However, like Buffalo Park, the path is shared with cyclists, so be sure to follow the leash rule to minimize user conflicts.

Once on trail, you and your dog are padding along a compacted surface, surrounded by striking limestone formations, grasses, ponderosa pines, scrub oaks, and Gambel oaks. Parts of your hike are quite shady, and in autumn, the shifting spectrum of the canopy is a real treat. Continue winding easterly throughout the hike. The canyon walls are a palette of buff, gray, and pink limestone, made easier to discern by the pretty cutouts and boulder outcroppings along your way.

At 0.9 mile, the trail turns south. Soon, you have a wetland in view—and it is a haven for all manner of birds: it is common to see redwing blackbirds perform vertical high wire acts on the cattails lining the pond here. Since this is a reclamation pond, it does not offer potable water,

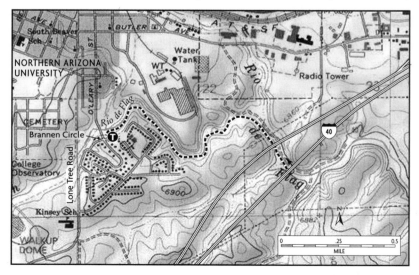

Delicate greenery dresses up Rio de Flag.

and you should limit your dog's splash breaks to the westernmost end of the hike at times when the stream is flowing. Pull out your field glasses and birding guide before turning the leash around and heading out the way you came.

7. Buffalo Park Urban Loop

Round trip: 2 miles
Hiking time: 1.5 hours
Difficulty: easy
High point: 7210 feet
Elevation change: 80 feet
Best: March through November
Map: Flagstaff West USGS
Contact: City of Flagstaff, Parks and Recreation Department, (928) 779-7690

Getting there: From Route 66 in Flagstaff, take Humphreys Road north to the T-intersection and head right (east) on Columbus one block to

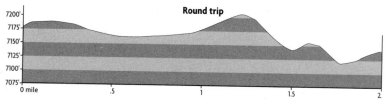

Beaver. Take Beaver left (north), then turn right on Forest. In just under a mile, take a left onto Gemini, follow the road as it curves, and drive into the signed parking area for Buffalo Park. The trailhead is through the stone and wood-faced arch, just past the buffalo statue.

Once your dog is watered and leashed—remember to take extra water since half of this loop hike is fully exposed—you are on your way. This trail loops through both meadow and forest atop a mesa nestled in the shadow of the San Francisco Peaks. Buffalo Park is busy at peak times, though not as busy as it could be. Mountain biking, though allowed, is unpopular here

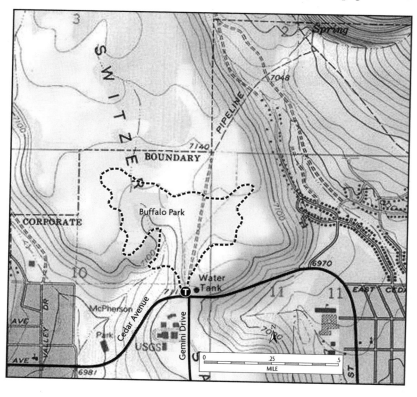

A broad meadow beneath the San Francisco Peaks along the Buffalo Park Urban Loop

thanks to the level trail. By heeding trail etiquette and leash rules, you and your dog will certainly enjoy this highly scenic, conditioning or maintenance hike just minutes from downtown Flagstaff.

You begin by heading straight (north) along the paw-pleasing, compacted path. You will pass the McMillan Mesa trail sign, then take the right (northeasterly) fork at the 0.1-mile mark to follow the Buffalo Park Urban Trail. You are actually following a trail that is shaped more like a splat than a circular loop, and the trail begins winding westerly through a shadier section of the meadow, with the San Francisco Peaks to your front and right. Your first convenient shady spot for a water or rest break for your dog comes at 0.7 mile, at the junction of this loop with the Utility Access road.

From here, you and your pooch jog northwest, before you begin to meander along a southeasterly and southwesterly heading. The ponderosa pines start crowding in on the trail at about the 1-mile mark. You take an unmarked right fork just past 1.6 miles, where you start winding downhill through a densely forested area. Pools form after rains and snowmelts, making this stretch of the loop a real treat for your dog in the spring. Lichen-encrusted boulders congregate in piles; tall pines always cast very cool, green shade, while the moodier oaks flush red and pink and orange in the fall. Take some playtime here, for your last quarter mile is an easy uphill saunter back to the parking lot, just west of the trailhead arch.

8. Little Spring to Bismarck Lake

Round trip: 2.5 miles
Hiking time: 2 hours
Difficulty: easy–moderate
High point: 8808 feet
Elevation change: 540 feet
Best: April through November
Maps: Humphreys Peak and White Horse Hills USGS
Contact: Coconino National Forest, Peaks Ranger Station, (928) 526-0866

Getting there: From Flagstaff, head north on State Hwy 180 for 19.4 miles and take a right at the second Forest Road 151 sign, just past mile point 235. Proceed 2.4 miles—you will pass a fork for FR 418—and take

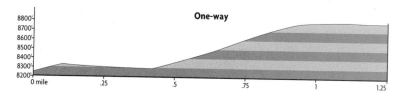

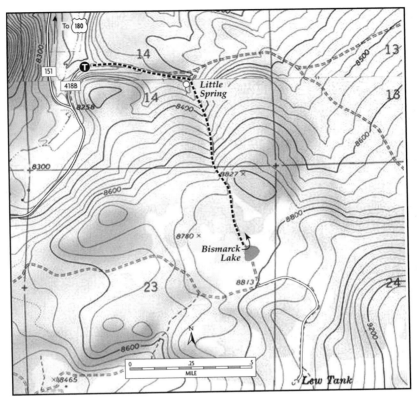

a left onto FR 418B. In 0.2 mile, you will come to a closed road. Park to the left here and do not block the gate. Pack in the additional drinking water you and your dog will need; once your dog is watered and leashed, go past the gate and follow the blocked road to the spring.

The wide two-track road takes you and your dog through a shady glen of spruce, ponderosa pine, and aspen. A gentle rise here foreshadows the climb ahead, but for now your path levels out at approximately 0.2 mile when the road leads you into a meadow. Though there are no signs on this trail, the only tricky part is finding the spring. Fortunately, even in dry years, it is fairly obvious to the careful observer. At the 0.4-mile mark, head right (southeast) directly across the meadow toward a thick clump of shrubs and a low hill; the spring is now routed through a pipe behind this glade. Be sure to treat any water you take from the spring. Cattle grazing is permitted on most public lands in Arizona, and giardia is always a threat.

A shock of green on a muted forest floor

Immediately behind the spring is a barrier; head around it and up the rise. For the next 0.4 mile, you and your dog climb steeply through the forest. The footpath is gentle to boot and paw, in spite of the steepness, though there is the occasional downed log to negotiate. During autmn, this hike offers stunning scenery. Many stands of elegant aspens, typically after the first frost, glow red, salmon pink, and burnt orange.

Your climb is a pleasant one, shady and scenic, with plenty of places throughout this portion of the trail to stop for water and rest breaks. You and your dog top off your climb at the 1-mile mark as the trail dead-ends at an old road. Take that path south (right). As you emerge from the forest into a broad alpine meadow (1.1 miles), you have a stunning view of the San Francisco Peaks. Head along the trail southwest to reach Bismarck Lake. Naturally, this being the arid Southwest, this lake can diminish to a tiny pond, or even dry up completely, in the summer. To see the lake at its fullest, time your hike after snowmelt in the spring, or after summer monsoons. Enjoy exploring this area—there are terrific picnic spots all around the meadow—and give your dog some splash time before turning back the way you came.

9. Walker Lake

Round trip: 1.25 miles
Hiking time: 1 hour
Difficulty: easy
High point: 8504 feet
Elevation change: 367 feet
Best: April through early November
Maps: Humphreys Peak, White Horse Hills, and Wing Mountain USGS
Contact: Coconino National Forest, Peaks Ranger Station,
(928) 526-0866

Getting there: From Flagstaff, take State Hwy 180 north for 19 miles. At just past mile point 235, take a right onto the unpaved road, marked both as upper Hart Prairie and FR 151, and continue 1.6 miles to FR 418, which is signed and forks left from FR 151. Check your odometer here. You will take the second left turn (it is unmarked) at just past 0.2 mile from FR 418. Follow this road to the 0.6-mile mark, then look uphill to your right to a barricaded road. Though not an official trail, hiking is permitted along this scenic path.

Once your dog is watered and leashed—pack in additional water since the lake may be dry—you are ready for a short climb and some fun exploring a forest oasis made by the remnant of an ancient cinder cone. You and your pooch begin by walking uphill on the old jeep road, now a wide path. The grade is gentle here, but constant, and the trail is a comfortable blend of compacted soil, pine duff, and cinder. Your way is partially shaded by a fairly thick forest of ponderosa pines and livened up here and there by stands of aspens, which glow red in the fall.

At just where the trail curves to the right (0.2 mile), you crest the lower lip of the cinder cone. Because a fire burned through this area several years ago, there is a large amount of slash at this bend; you will either

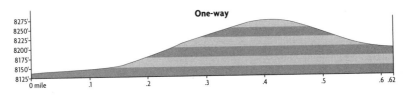

A sliver of Walker Lake's ephemeral waters mirrors the surrounding meadow and forest.

have to navigate over some logs or scale the small hill to the right to join up with the road past that bend—it is easy to pick up the trail again in about 25 yards by heading northeast.

From here, you have a terrific view of the lake (or lakebed if the lake is dry). This area is so placid that it is hard to imagine that this was once a lake of fire. Now, when the lake is full—spring snowmelt is the best time to visit here—frogs sing at a frenzied pitch, birds flit amongst the trees lining the football field–sized basin, and deer occasionally meander to the shore from their forest cover.

You now have a choice of taking the fork of the trail that leads

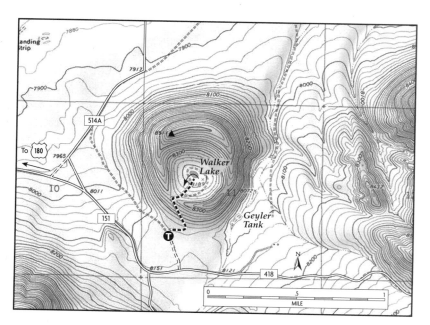

directly to the lake or continuing to follow the road eastward to circumnavigate more of the basin at tree line. Of course, doing both adds to the fun of your cool, forest hike before turning the leash around and leaving the way you came.

10. Red Mountain

Round trip: 2.5 miles
Hiking time: 2 hours
Difficulty: easy
High point: 7108 feet
Elevation gain: 376 feet
Best: April through November
Map: Ebert Mountain USGS
Contact: Coconino National Forest, Peaks Ranger Station,
 (928) 526-0866
Note: This hike is best suited for those with smaller dogs, as dogs
 will have to be assisted up a stepladder.

Getting there: Getting to the trailhead is simple. From Flagstaff, take State Hwy 180 north toward the Grand Canyon about 30 miles to just before mile point 247. You will see a sign for the Red Mountain trailhead; turn left onto the well-graded gravel road and continue to the end of the road to park at the signed trailhead. Once your dog is watered and leashed—pack in additional water, as none is routinely available on this trail—proceed past the information kiosk to the footpath.

You and your dog will enjoy this shady hike to a highly unusual geological feature, the heart of a cinder cone estimated to be about three quarters of a million years old. Cinder cones are common in this region, but this one has crumbled and eroded in a way that makes the mountain look as though a cross section has been scooped away. The trail ends at

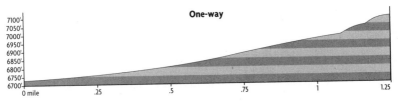

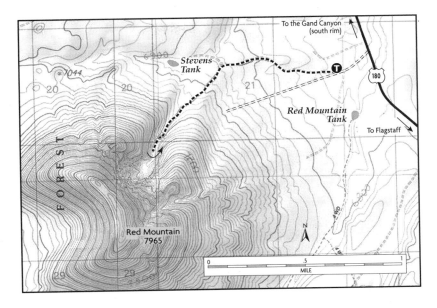

the base of this cone, and you can explore part of the area inside this ancient volcano.

The wide, compacted-earth footpath heads west from the trailhead toward Red Mountain, which hovers above tree line and winks at you through the taller trees throughout your hike. You and your dog wind steadily uphill through pinyon-juniper woodland into a ponderosa pine forest as you journey into the volcano.

Once a sprawling maze of poorly marked and informal-use trails, this now well-maintained path winds steadily toward the mountain's heart. At the 0.8-mile mark, the trail jogs south (left); markers direct you into a wash. Avoid this trail during rains; as with all washes in the Southwest, flash floods pose a danger during storms.

Shortly, two giant ponderosa pines, which form a natural archway, welcome you into an eerie landscape of twisted and colorful volcanic rock forms. Before the 1.2-mile mark, you come upon a stepladder, which takes you into the base of the cinder cone—dogs will most likely need assistance. Take some time for a quick rest break and exploration of this highly unusual area before heading out the way you came.

Opposite: Ponderous boulders of frozen fire in repose at the foot of Red Mountain's collapsed cinder cone

11. Weatherford

Round trip: 10 to 19 miles
Hiking time: 6 to 10 hours
Difficulty: difficult
High point: 12,633 feet
Elevation change: 3200 feet
Best: April through November
Map: Humphreys Peak USGS
Contact: Coconino National Forest, Peaks Ranger Station,
(928) 526-0866
Notes: Forest Road 420 is closed in winter; call the ranger station for
driving and hiking conditions. Also, avoid this trail when
summer storms and lightning are predicted.

Getting there: From Flagstaff, take State Hwy 180 north approximately
5 miles to Schultz Pass Road (also known as Forest Road 420); turn right
(east). At the junction with FR 557, veer left to stay on FR 420 to arrive
at the trailhead in 6 miles. Park on the right, near Schultz Tank; the
trailhead is across FR 420. Once your dog is watered and leashed, head
north from the parking area to pick up your path.

The Weatherford Trail 102 takes you to within barking distance of the
roof of Arizona and lies almost entirely within the highly scenic Kachina
Peaks Wilderness Area. The path is open to hiking and horseback riding
only—and no horses are allowed beyond Doyle Saddle—so this remains
a remote trail, in spite of convenient access from Flagstaff. Since some of
this San Francisco Peaks trail is above tree line, watch summer temperatures carefully when planning your trip and pack in extra water.

The trail bed itself is an old toll road, which means you and your dog
have a good walking surface with a relatively gentle incline throughout
much of this long day hike through mixed conifer and aspen forests and
broad alpine meadows.

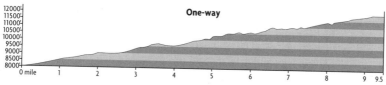

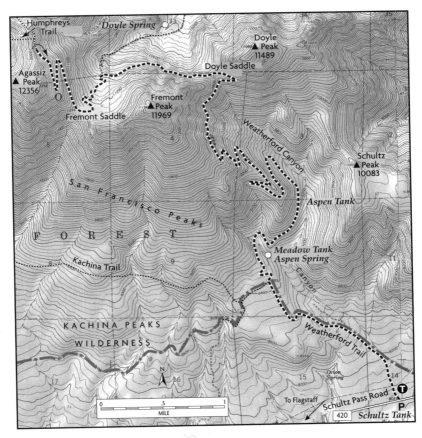

You cross a gas pipeline road less than 0.1 mile from the trailhead. Blazed paths spur off to the right and left; continue north/northwest on the main track. At the fork at 0.7 mile, stay left to continue on the Weatherford Trail, and in no time, you duck under the cool cover of the forest. In spring and summer, the aspens cast a chartreuse glow. After the first frost, generally in early October, the woods glint with autumn's showiest hues. Your dog won't need to signal you when the elks are bugling in the fall—even humans can hear the bulls' plaintive mating cries for many miles. As you continue along the eastern side of the Peaks, you will enjoy some stellar views bracketed to the south by the red rocks of Sedona and, closer in, by Schultz Peak to your north.

Along your northwesterly route toward Doyle Saddle and Fremont Peak, at 1.7 miles, you intersect the Kachina Trail to the left; veer right

Aspen groves and autumn color abound throughout the Kachina Peaks Wilderness.

to stay on the Weatherford Trail. More switchbacks have you skirting Weatherford Canyon to the east under the watchful eye of Fremont and Doyle Peaks. At 5 miles you reach Doyle Saddle. Aspens do not march as high as this, and in fact, the vegetation thins considerably, reminding you that you are, after all, still in the arid Southwest.

Many prefer to turn around here, but if you are well stocked with water and your dog's tail is still wagging, more lovely views and cool shade lie ahead. A level section is in store after you have traversed a boulderfall on Fremont Peak and then turned west again. Spruces and bristlecone pines dominate the landscape for a while, lending choice spots for a shade break with your dog.

At 6.5 miles you come to a trail junction with the Inner Basin Trail to the northeast. To protect endangered and endemic plants, off-trail exploration is prohibited above this point. Continue your gentle uphill climb by staying left. As you ascend above tree line enjoy views to the north stretching as far as the pastel sands of the Painted Desert. At just past 8.7 miles, the Weatherford Trail bumps into the Humphreys Trail. If your supplies of energy, water, tail wags, and time are all hunky dory, add another 1.5 miles to your round trip by continuing straight (north) along the much steeper Humphreys Trail to reach Mt. Humphreys, the highest point in Arizona. When you are ready to go, turn the leash around and head south, back the way you came.

12. Sandys Canyon to Walnut Canyon

Round trip: 7.2 miles
Hiking time: 4 hours
Difficulty: easy–moderate
High point: 6853 feet
Elevation change: 300 feet
Best: April through November
Maps: Lower Lake Mary and Flagstaff East USGS
Contact: Coconino National Forest, Mormon Lake Ranger Station, (928) 774-1147

Getting there: From Flagstaff, take the Lake Mary Road 5.5 miles south. Cross a cattle guard and take an immediate left onto the well-graded

gravel road. Pass Canyon Vista Campground to park in just under 0.25 mile at the end of the road. Once your dog is watered and leashed—remember to pack in additional water—head north from the parking area onto the tree-lined path. Within 400 feet, there is a signed junction; take a left for the Sandys Canyon Trail 137.

This scenic trail leads you and your dog through mountain meadows, lush canyons, and cool, tree-covered ridges. The path is initially a comfortable and compacted forest floor. Your northwest heading ultimately leads you to the lip of Sandys Canyon, but the great views start at the trailhead and rarely let up. The San Francisco Peaks make a couple of grand entrances at different viewpoints along this hike, and the unusual cliffs and red rock formations of Walnut Canyon are a delight.

Within 0.5 mile, you start a moderate descent. Here, oaks and aspens start to crowd into the ponderosa pine forest, glinting gold and red in autumn. The trail jogs to the left, northeasterly, at the bottom of the canyon (0.8 mile), and you are now trekking through the Walnut Creek drainage, which along this stretch is typically dry. After snowmelt and rains, your dog will be able to cool her pads when you cross the streambed at 0.9 mile.

At 1.4 miles, you arrive at a signed trail junction at the end of the Sandys Canyon Trail proper. For a beautiful walk into Walnut Canyon, continue north (straight), following the signs for the Arizona Trail. You travel along an old jeep road here for a mile through an exposed mountain meadow, so be sure you have sun protection and take water breaks with your dog. The trail forks at just before 2.2 miles; head right (northeast) toward a swooping, eastward bend in the canyon. The cliff walls sport petrified sand dunes, beautiful rock formations reminiscent of pulled taffy. At just past 2.25 miles, turn right (east) to take a secondary trail into Walnut Canyon. A cave on your left at 2.4 miles makes a shady break spot. Be sure to check that a sun-drunk snake did not have the same idea—watch where hands and curious dog noses go.

Shortly, the canyon narrows where there is an interpretive sign and a sign cautioning against camping and fires in the area. You roll in and around the streambed—splash, anyone?—along a much shadier trail thanks to the cliff walls and thicker canopy of the alligator junipers, Gambel oaks, aspens, and ponderosa pines crowding the canyon bottoms. You will see on the outcroppings more than one tree doing an improbable balancing act, poised for a swan dive into the creek—it is a beautiful and bizarre setting. Occasionally, the path turns sandy along the creek, but always reverts back to a comfortable padding surface.

You come to another cave, this time to the right of the trail, at 2.6 miles. Explore its cool environs with caution. You continue along in the drainage for nearly a mile until the path takes you away from the creek through a pretty glen. Just beyond, at the 3.6-mile mark, the trail ends with no fanfare. Enjoy a shady break here or along Walnut Creek before turning the leash around and heading out the way you came. Note that

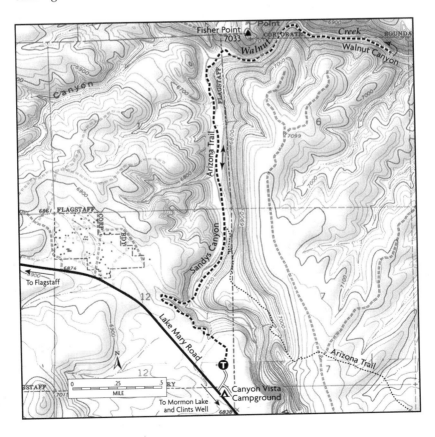

The curvy architecture of wind, water, and deposition is a delight in Walnut Canyon.

on your way back, at the last signed junction, you follow the sign that points to the Canyon Vista parking area to return to the trailhead (it is not marked as the Sandys Canyon trailhead).

13. Hutch Mountain to Gooseberry Spring

Round trip: 4 miles
Hiking time: 3 hours
Difficulty: easy–moderate
High point: 8412 feet
Elevation change: 430 feet
Best: April through November
Map: Hutch Mountain USGS
Contact: Coconino National Forest, Mormon Lake Ranger Station, (928) 774-1147

Getting there: From Flagstaff, take Lake Mary Road 33 miles south to mile point 311; turn left (east) onto Forest Road 135. This often rutted road is best tackled with a high-clearance vehicle. Continue on FR 135 past a leftward fork, which is FR 135C; take the second left fork, signed FR 135B. Follow FR 135B for 1.5 miles and park where the road ends at the gate, but do not block the gate. Once your dog is watered and leashed

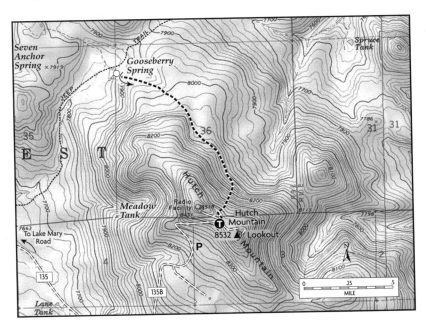

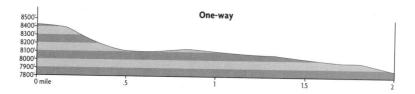

(pack in water in case the spring is dry, and plan to purify any water you take from the spring), walk uphill along the road beyond the gate for 0.1 mile. Where the road makes a wide bend to the right, look down to your left—this is the trail, though it is unmarked.

You and your dog first make a short, rocky, and moderately steep scramble down the north face of Hutch Mountain. Before taking the plunge, enjoy the views of the San Francisco Peaks and Anderson Mesa—once you are on your way, the views recede behind the mature fir, spruce, and aspen trees that shade your path.

Your heading is initially due north as you switchback down the mountain. The path is narrow and somewhat rocky, so take your time. At just past the 0.3-mile mark, the trail levels out and follows FR 92D in a general northwesterly heading. From here and up until the 1.3-mile mark,

The frosted crown of the San Francisco Peaks as seen before the plunge from Hutch Mountain.

there are many excellent places to break when your dog is ready for a drink in the shade. After this point, you are traversing exposed meadows. Even at 8000 feet, you should take care that you and your dog do not become dehydrated.

You reach Gooseberry Spring after passing a tank on your right—the valley is pretty in both spring and fall during wet years, when wildflowers put on the Ritz. Take a left from the road (heading southwest) to get to the spring, now boxed but still accessible. As always, purify first any water you drink from the spring. Explore the shady edges of this scenic mountain meadow before leaving the way you came.

14. Route 66

Round trip: 1.5 miles
Hiking time: 1 hour
Difficulty: easy
High point: 7200 feet
Elevation change: 65 feet
Best: March through November
Map: Parks USGS
Contact: Kaibab National Forest, Williams Visitor Center,
(800) 863-0546 or (928) 635-4061

Getting there: Take Interstate 40 about 17 miles west from Flagstaff to Parks. Take exit 178, turn right and proceed to the next intersection. Check your odometer and take a right (east) here onto old Route 66. Before the 1-mile mark, just past a cattle guard, you will see a pullout on your left with a wooden barricade and a sign. This is the trailhead.

Once your dog is watered and leashed, you are ready to "get your kicks on Route 66."

This short but sweet hiking trail is aptly called a "ghost road," and is made up of the area's now-defunct, 1931 section of the fabled Route 66,

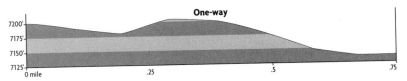

a 2000-mile auto route that is inseparable from twentieth century Western folklore. Route 66 is a truly pleasant stroll for you and a nice conditioning trail for your dog, thanks to the mixture of surfaces. Be sure to pack in all the water you need, since none is available along your way.

As you and your pooch first set out, the path gently rolls southwest and downhill on a wide swath of loose gravel and grasses. The parklike, ponderosa pine forest casts dappled shade along your entire route, making for cool spring and fall outings and pleasantly warm summer jaunts. Bits of concrete lying off to the side of the path and this trail's arrow-straight configuration are all that initially indicate the original roadway. Soon, though, history crowds in and a concrete culvert here or a bit of unbroken roadway there emerges. Occasionally, you can glimpse the faint traces of an even older Route 66 right-of-way, from 1921, to the side of the path.

Just past the 0.5-mile mark, you come upon a rustic and disused Forest Service spring house which once supplied water for a campground. The spring house is nestled south of the trail in a cluster of oaks and it is a particularly pretty spot in October, after the first frost, when fall colors steal into the canopy of this otherwise evergreen forest.

The trail continues another quarter mile, almost to the intersection of Parks Road and present-day Route 66. At the terminus, you will see

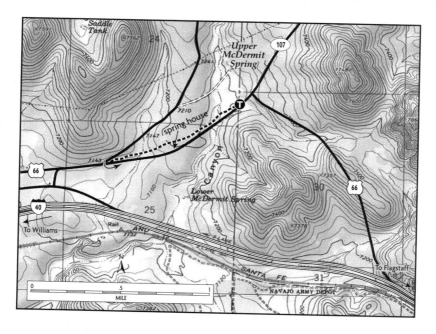

An old Forest Service spring house along Route 66

remnants of concrete culverts that mark where the 1931 section and the 1921 section converged. Explore the 1921 route a bit before turning Fido's leash around and heading back the way you came.

15. Keyhole Sink

Round trip: 1.5 miles
Hiking time: 1 hour
Difficulty: easy
High point: 7034 feet
Elevation change: 84 feet
Best: April through November
Map: Parks USGS
Contact: Kaibab National Forest, Williams Ranger Station,
(928) 635-4061

Getting there: From Flagstaff, take Interstate 40 west for approximately 24 miles to exit 171. After you exit, turn right (east) onto Historic Route 66. In 2 miles, park on the right at the signed lot for the Oak Hill Snow

Play area. The trail is on the north side of Route 66, across the road from the parking lot. As with all trails in the arid Southwest, you should pack your drinking water in and use sun protection. Once your dog is watered and leashed, cross Route 66 to the gated trailhead.

Close the gate behind you and you are on your way on Keyhole Sink Trail 114. There is a lot on this hike for your dog (and her human companion) to enjoy: spring and autumn, after snowmelts and rains, Keyhole Sink is a pretty pool in the heart of the box canyon. The trail's namesake "sink" feeds a lush, green oasis that, when it holds water, is visited by deer, a plethora of woodland birds, butterflies, and spadefoot toads.

Your path into the box canyon is an easy hike along a comfortable and compacted forest floor. You and your dog wind northwest through a shady ponderosa pine and alligator juniper forest. Thanks to the double life of this trail—this is a popular cross-country skiing trail in winter—there are plenty of blue triangles on trees that keep you heading the right direction should mud or duff obscure the footpath.

It is apparent that you are heading to a gem of a canyon almost immediately upon setting out. Colorful, lichen-splattered boulders creep toward the trail starting at the 0.25 mile mark, foreshadowing scenic outcroppings at 0.5 mile just as the trail turns more northeast. A graceful stand of young aspens that heralds the edge of the canyon flushes gold and red in the fall. Canyon walls rise up, sheer and black against the crumbling, living boulders in the surrounds.

The Keyhole Sink was formed by lava deposition and subsequently, waters carved a small basin at the heart of the tiny box canyon. The trail leads you through a gate; there is a registration book here, just past the 0.6-mile mark. Thousand-year-old rock art, or petroglyphs, dot the canyon walls and low-lying boulders inside the canyon, which you can freely explore once past the gate. While your dog cools her pads, some modest bouldering will take you in for a closer look at the petroglyphs, but do not disturb them.

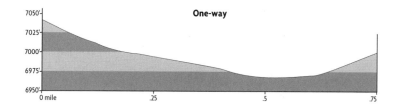

A pool at the heart of Keyhole Sink

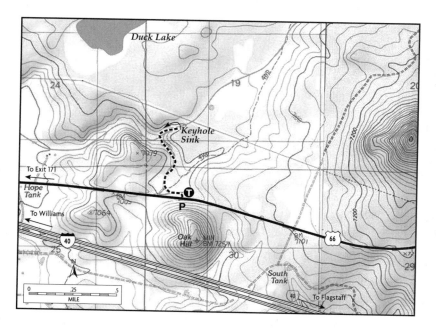

Given the brambles and the more open environs within the canyon, enjoy the pool, marvel at the petroglyphs, then save your rest and water breaks for the many flat areas under the tall ponderosas that surround the trail on your way in or out.

SYCAMORE CANYON WILDERNESS

16. Sycamore Rim Loop

Round trip: 11.4 miles
Hiking time: 5.5 hours
Difficulty: moderate
High point: 7121 feet
Elevation change: 887 feet
Best: April through November
Maps: White Horse Lake and Sycamore Point USGS
Contact: Kaibab National Forest, Williams Ranger Station, (928) 635-8200; Williams/Forest Service Visitor Center, (928) 635-4061 or (800) 863-0546

Getting there: To get there from Flagstaff, take Interstate 40 west about 30 miles to Garland Prairie Road. Exit south (left); once you've passed under the freeway, go over the railroad tracks and take an immediate left onto Forest Road 141. After several miles the road forks with FR 140; stay left on FR 141. At the fork with FR 109, go right on FR 109, then turn left to the Pomeroy Tanks trailhead. Pack in plenty of water for this long,

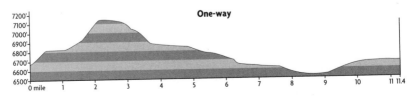

partly exposed canyon trail. Once you have watered and leashed your dog, head east from the trailhead through the gate next to the rest rooms.

This pleasant, 11.4-mile loop is a terrific way for you and your dog to enjoy the shady forests, rugged canyons, and natural, ephemeral pools tucked just above the lip of the Sycamore Canyon Wilderness Area. Your route on Sycamore Rim Loop 45 is a clockwise tour starting from the Pomeroy trailhead. You begin on a comfortable, compacted forest floor, shaded by towering ponderosa pines, Gambel oaks, and alligator junipers—autumn is cool and lovely here.

A gorge at 0.2 mile offers your first glimpse of Pomeroy Tanks, a pretty chain of natural reservoirs. Follow the trail north through and around the tanks, noting their striking forms, and rolling up and down on rocky staircases interspersed with loose gravel. There can be water here year-round, but naturally the best splash time for your dog is after snowmelt and summer rains.

You will pass the Overland Road junction at 0.6 mile to enter a broad, sunny meadow. Cairns guide you where the trail is faint—it is likely, though, that your dog will have sniffed out the correct path.

You cross FR 113 at 0.9 mile and duck under the forest canopy again.

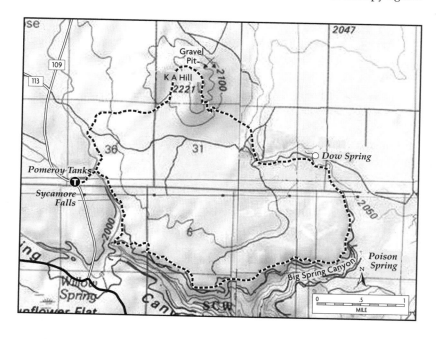

Funky boulder outcrops keep you and your dog company on your way through the Pomeroy Tanks.

You and your dog come to an especially pretty spot on your ascent (just past 2 miles) where there are close trees and plenty of shady, flat areas to take a water break. Your climb intensifies here as you and Fido make your way to the top of KA Hill—to the northeast, you have a great view of the stately San Francisco Peaks. When you are ready to continue the loop, follow the switchbacks down to the next trailhead, at FR 56. The walking is easy along the rest of the route.

Dow Spring is your next stop. Past this trailhead, your path turns first south, then west, to follow the canyon rim. The views are magnificent: soft folds of green belie the rugged nature of Sycamore Canyon. This 5-mile segment of your route offers only intermittent shade until Sycamore Falls, an area known to climbers who flock to the sheer walls of this gorge at Paradise Forks. On warm days, let your dog soak in the shade where you find it, and take plenty of water breaks. By the time you make your final approach to Paradise Forks, you are back under the cool pines. This is a pretty place to explore with your dog after snowmelt or rains, and you should give her a chance to cool her pads before making your northward, 1.2-mile jaunt back to Pomeroy trailhead—and home.

17. Sycamore Basin

Round trip: 6 miles
Hiking time: 3.5 hours
Difficulty: easy
High point: 4718 feet
Elevation change: 205 feet
Best: September through May
Maps: Sycamore Basin USGS; Sycamore Canyon Wilderness Map
Contact: Coconino National Forest, Red Rocks Ranger Station, (928) 282-4119
Note: Sections of this trail experience flooding after heavy rains; check trail conditions with the ranger before heading out.

Getting there: From Flagstaff, take Interstate 40 west for 30 miles; take exit 165 (Williams) and turn left. Drive through town and turn left on Fourth Street, which is also signed as Perkinsville Road and County Road 73. You will continue on this road for just over 24 miles; take the left

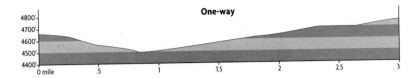

fork at Forest Road 492 for 3.2 miles. Turn right onto FR 354 and check your odometer. Proceed 2.4 miles to turn left onto unsigned FR 181. Stay on FR 181 for 13.4 miles. You will see a tiny marker on the right for Trails 63 and 66, as well as a gate; this is your trailhead for Sycamore Basin Trail 63.

The long drive to this short hike pays off in a remote wilderness experience and scenic red rock views that you can enjoy with your dog. Once you have watered and leashed your dog—and be sure you have packed in plenty of water for this exposed trail—head through the gate and into the Sycamore Canyon Wilderness Area. The fairly level trail follows a slightly winding, northeasterly heading and you immediately come upon a sign that directs you ahead to Sycamore Basin, Cow Flat, and the Taylor Cabin Trail. Cross a wash—unless it has rained recently it will probably be dry— and follow the path as it dips down gently into the basin.

If it was not for the evergreen pinyons and junipers, the scenery would make you think you were either wearing rose-colored glasses or had fallen through a wormhole to Mars. Red rocks at the basin, fading to pink and a rouge-colored tan in the upper bands of the surrounding cliffs, are a sensory paradox—this desert monochrome is as striking as it is hypnotic. The landscape is in fact quite lush, as the cactus wrens, golden eagles, rattlesnakes, lizards, and mountain lions could tell you—scrub oaks, grasses, agaves, yuccas, prickly pears, chollas, and wildflowers cluster all about. The larger biomasses—that is, shade-bearing trees—are sustained primarily near the washes.

At just over 0.3 mile, you and your dog cross another major washbed tiled with slickrock. There are cairns to guide you, but the trail is obvious and your heading is still northeast. At 1 mile, you confront a labyrinthine wash system—keep your northeast heading and you will pick up the trail. Just past this point, there are some ancient junipers—and, oddly enough, an occasional, lonely ponderosa pine as well—shading some level areas where you can enjoy a long break out of the sun with your dog.

From this point on, several of the minor washes you cross have some sandy stretches, but they are very brief and should not steal your attention away from the beautiful, craggy outcroppings that line the washbeds. At 1.25 miles, there is a really funky wash system where the trail seems obliterated; here you must continue east to pick up the trail, which will correct back to the northeast heading in no time.

At 1.6 miles, you come to the Cross D Tank, which is signed, and a quaint, juniper-post corral. Pass the trail junction to Yew Thicket Trail 52 at 2 miles and continue northeast. Beginning at Cross D Tank, a cockscomb mountain comes into view to your right (east) and its red, spiky eminence is more impressive the further you travel into Sycamore Basin.

You and your dog continue to wander through washes (and the sparse shade they offer) and start a gentle climb to the terminus. You reach a small ridge at 3 miles with terrific views—gaze southwest at the path you

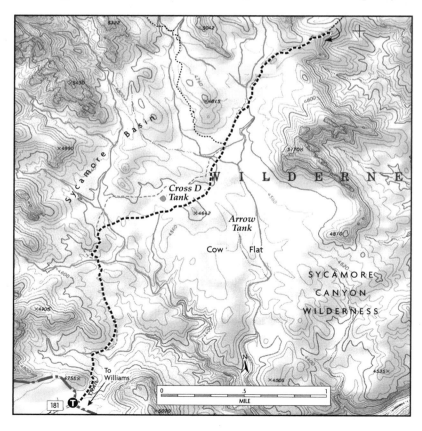

In Sycamore Basin, wildflowers and cacti adorn an already showy red rock landscape.

have taken to this point and when you are ready, turn the leash around and head back.

18. Geronimo Spring

Round trip: 4 miles
Hiking time: 3 hours
Difficulty: moderate–difficult
High point: 6670 feet
Elevation change: 1411 feet
Best: April through November
Map: Sycamore Point USGS; Sycamore Canyon Wilderness Map
Contact: Coconino National Forest, Peaks Ranger Station,
(928) 526-0866

Getting there: From Flagstaff, take Route 66 west for 2.6 miles, turning left onto the Woody Mountain Road (you will see a sign directing you to the Flagstaff Arboretum), which is also Forest Road 231. Check your odometer here. Take FR 231 for 14 miles—13 miles of that is a well-maintained

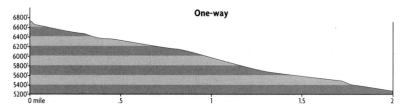

unpaved surface, but the remaining roads require high-clearance vehicles. At 14 miles, you will come to FR 538; turn right and go 5.7 miles to a fork. Take FR 538E to the right and follow it 0.4 mile. When you see the sign for Dorsey Spring to the left, continue straight—the road is now signed as 538G—for 1 mile. At the sign for Kelsey Trail Road, take a left; the road ends in 0.4 mile at your trailhead.

Once your dog is watered, point her leash downhill and head north through the gate. Your trail to Geronimo Spring first follows the same path as the Kelsey and Little LO Trails. Remember to pack in water in case the springs are dry and always purify what you take from springs if they are running.

You will cross into Sycamore Canyon Wilderness right away. This is an enchanting place, with three fairly reliable springs that lush up this desert montane forest nicely. Your path through this beautiful woodland is steep in places, but offers access to water when the springs are running, plenty of shade, and some nice views of Sycamore Canyon. In the spring, wildflowers add a sheen of yellow and purple to the meadows, while autumn's reds blaze through the canopy wherever oaks have taken hold.

Since setting out, you and your dog have been winding steadily downhill. You quickly come upon Kelsey Spring at 0.2 mile, where the trail levels out briefly. The spring is to the right of the trail and is signed, but you likely will not need to scan the area for a sign because of the burst of green that the spring feeds in all but the driest of times. Your path follows the spring's watercourse briefly—the first treat for your hard-playing trail dog—then turns southeast and downhill again, ducking under heavier forest cover.

Along this trail you will notice a number of camping sites, all of which are located more than 200 feet (required in wilderness to help preserve them) from the springs. One such cluster of old fire rings and conveniently situated downed logs (terrific for a quick rest and water break, particularly on your way back up the mountain) is located at the 0.6 mile mark. On your way downhill, a great break point comes at 1 mile, where

Babes Hole Spring is located. This area has a primitive "rest area" next to a tower of rocks where the spring used to bubble up (covered now for safety since the spring is piped). By now, you and Fido are heading north-west—your orientation for the rest of this hike.

You roll in and out of washes—typically dry except directly after rains—at the 0.75 and 0.8 mile marks. From here through mile 1.3, en-joy brief but beautiful vistas of Sycamore Canyon: impressionistic strata of red, buff, pink, and gray light up the tree-covered canyon walls.

At 1.1 miles, you reach the junction for Kelsey Trail 3 (left) and Little LO Trail 6; you take the rightward fork to continue to Geronimo Spring. The switchbacks tighten up and occasionally the path gets loose and rocky, so mind your footing. Though ponderosa pines, Douglas-firs, ju-nipers, and oaks cast plenty of shade on this hike, do not forget sun pro-tection; the forest is quite open for some stretches, and occasionally, the path is totally exposed. During the last 0.3 mile, the forest cover deep-ens, the light taking on a pleasing green glow. Abrupt drops alternate with level stretches until you bottom out at 1.8 miles.

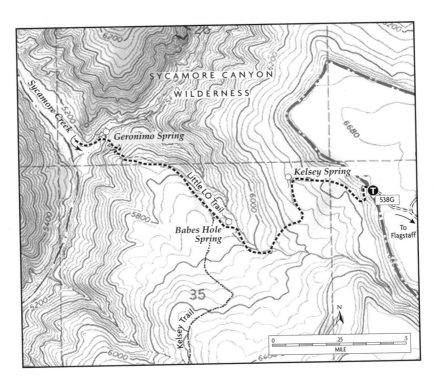

When flowing, Geronimo Spring makes a cool, paw-pleasing, eye-catching oasis.

Geronimo Spring is on your left, its waters feeding an oasis of irises and mosses. When the spring is flowing, the stream runs southwest toward the canyon. If you follow the watercourse, you come to some campsites. Following the trail to the right leads you into Sycamore Canyon, where you can explore, hopping boulders and—if you and your dog are lucky—wading in this ephemeral stretch of Sycamore Creek to your heart's content. All around are pretty places to recharge your batteries and get your dog's tail wagging again before heading out the way you came.

Intrepid hiker-dog teams who want either an easy backpacking trip or a longer day hike might want to turn south at the junction of Little LO and Kelsey Trails. Continue on Kelsey 2.3 miles to Dorsey Spring and 3.2 more miles to Winter Cabin Spring, where you will turn east and take Hog Hill Trail 133 to get back to FR 538G (see Hikes 19 and 20). You simply hike FR 538G north-northwest, past Casner Tank and in the shadow of Red Hill, back to the Kelsey trailhead when you emerge from Hog Hill.

In addition to topos, a Sycamore Canyon Wilderness Area map is useful for this 9.5-mile loop.

19. Dorsey Spring

Round trip: 5 miles
Hiking time: 3.5 hours
Difficulty: moderate
High point: 6932
Elevation gain: 800
Best: April through November
Map: Sycamore Point USGS; Sycamore Canyon Wilderness Map
Contact: Coconino National Forest, Peaks Ranger Station,
    (928) 526-0866

Getting there: From Flagstaff, take old Route 66 west for 2.6 miles, turning left onto Mountain Road (you will see a sign directing you to the Flagstaff Arboretum), which is also Forest Road 231. Check your odometer here. Follow FR 231 south for 14 miles—13 miles of that is a well-maintained unpaved surface, but the remaining roads require high clearance vehicles. At 14 miles, you will come to FR 538; turn right and go 5.7 miles to a fork. Take FR 538E to the right and follow it 0.4 mile. At the sign for Dorsey Spring, follow that road left for approximately 0.25 mile. The road ends at the trailhead.

Well over half of this fairly remote trail is in the Sycamore Canyon Wilderness, which means it is open only to hiking and horseback riding past the wilderness boundary at 0.8 mile. You should plan on taking along your drinking water since the spring can be dry; in the happy event that the water is running, purify what you take to drink while your dog enjoys a splash.

Once your dog is watered and leashed up, take the path out of the parking circle. Dorsey Spring Trail 7 shares a trailhead with the Hog Hill

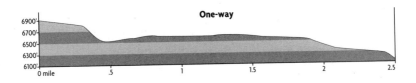

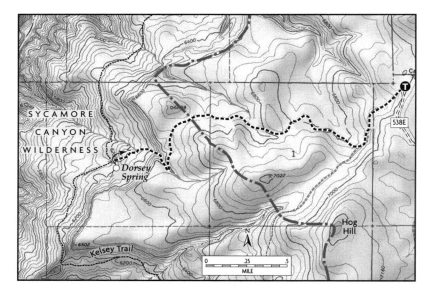

Trail, and initially you and your dog follow an old road, so the path is somewhat rocky, wide, and exposed. You come to an unsigned fork at 0.25 mile—you will see an old gatepost—Hog Hill continues straight and the Dorsey Spring Trail takes off to the right (westerly). A winding path takes you through a lovely, mixed-age pine-juniper-oak forest, parts of which are real showstoppers in autumn: from saplings to centenarians, oaks drape the canopy and forest floor with fall color like a lavish, shimmering veil. Wildflowers wave their purples, fuscias, whites, and golds silently throughout the spring, and hardy brambles—a cacophony of green—line the washes and canyon.

From the Hog Hill junction, a somewhat loose and rocky trail bed turns into a comfortable, compacted floor for most of your route—good news for your dog's pads. The wilderness boundary at 0.8 mile is marked by a Z-gate. The many parklike sections of this hike are interspersed by ponderosa pines and Gambel oaks, and a venerable stand of lovely old alligator junipers provides welcome shade at 1.75 miles.

You cross a scenic and lush gorge just past 1.8 miles. The path is faint and there are no cairns, so be sure to take a right (northwest) to pick up the path, which now follows the drainage for a time. You and your dog will enjoy boulder hopping here, and the path briefly drops more steeply. You cross the gorge four more times before the path levels and turns southwest away from the drainage.

Just before 2.25 miles, giant boulders frame a view of Sycamore Canyon. The trail draws you and your dog downhill again along an increasingly lush path: beautiful irises, vines, and grasses pop up around Dorsey Spring when it is running. If you follow the trickle from the piped spring, to the southwest, water pools and meanders invitingly. This is a fun area to explore, with plenty of level ground and shade; in fact, a number of campsites are located beyond the regulation 200 feet from the spring. To continue on the trail, however, return to the spring and go downhill (northwest) along the faint path so that the spring is behind you and to your left. You will come upon more dispersed camping or break spots here.

In just under 0.1 mile from the spring, you come to the trail junction with Kelsey Trail 3. Extend your hike by making an 8-mile mini-loop with the Kelsey and Hog Hill Trails (see Hike 20), or point the leash uphill when you are ready to leave the canyon and cool pines behind.

Gambel oaks shimmer along the Dorsey Spring Trail.

20. Hog Hill to Winter Cabin Spring

Round trip: 4.8 miles
Hiking time: 3 hours
Difficulty: moderate
High point: 7000 feet
Elevation change: 750 feet
Best: April through November
Map: Sycamore Point USGS; Sycamore Canyon Wilderness Map
Contact: Coconino National Forest, Peaks Ranger Station,
     (928) 526-0866

Getting there: From Flagstaff, take Route 66 west for 2.6 miles, turning left onto the Woody Mountain Road (you will see a sign directing you to the Flagstaff Arboretum), which is also Forest Road 231. Check your odometer here. Take FR 231 for 14 miles—13 miles of that is a well maintained unpaved surface, but the remaining roads require high-clearance vehicles. At 14 miles, you will come to FR 538; turn right and go 5.7 miles to a fork. Take FR 538E to the right and follow it 0.4 mile. At the sign for Dorsey Spring, follow that road left for approximately 0.25 mile. The road ends at the trailhead.

Starting left of the trailhead parking area, trek southward once your dog is watered and leashed. Remember to pack in your drinking water, as the spring at the hike's terminus may not be running. The path is a combination of cinder and compacted forest floor, part of which once was an old jeep road—you will encounter some loose, rocky areas, but overall this is a comfortable walking surface. Hog Hill Trail 133 narrows to a faint footpath every now and then, and occasionally you follow hoof prints, since this wilderness trail allows both hiking and horseback riding.

You do not scale the top of Hog Hill on this trail; instead, you climb

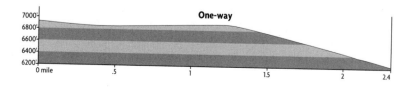

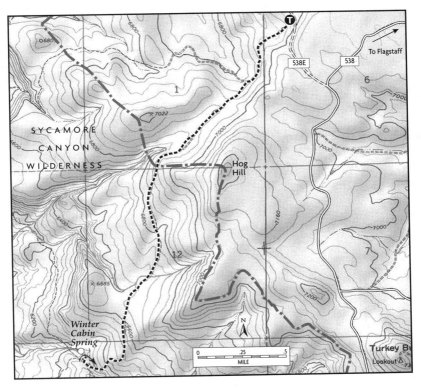

down toward Sycamore Canyon to Winter Cabin Spring on Hog Hill's sprawling western flank, sheltered by the ponderosa pine, Gambel oak, and alligator juniper trees that live companionably here. Initially, the trail is fairly level and exposed. You and your dog come to an unsigned junction at 0.25 mile—you will see a decrepit gatepost—the rightward path is the Dorsey Spring Trail, but you lead the leash left to stay on Hog Hill Trail. At 0.8 mile, you cross into the Sycamore Canyon Wilderness. The overstory claims more of the sky here, and the path narrows. Soon, past the 1-mile mark, you are treated to pretty views of Sycamore Canyon's western face through a screen of trees on your right. Tall spires, seemingly delicate as confections, stretch up from the canyon floor in layers of red, pink, beige, gray, and taupe.

The trail meanders briefly through pockets of high desert and pinyon-juniper forest, and you and your dog happen upon scrub oaks, agaves, cacti, and the characteristic boulder outcroppings whose crevices these plants love. Desert and trail blur a bit here, so keep to your southward

A watery death, a dry grave

heading and watch for cairns. You cross two washes (at 1.3 and 1.6 miles), then zig west and zag southwest on the faint footpath. Soon, though, you duck back under a pine-oak forest and into cool shade as you make your final descent toward Winter Cabin Spring. Though you are back under the forest canopy, you will not miss out on stunning views: at 2 miles, you are treated to a gorgeous canyon vista, and closer in, to pretty and lushly vegetated outcroppings.

For a short stretch, you and your dog vault downhill as the trail heads west and crosses a wash. There is a trail junction at 2.4 miles; from here, you can see the remains of Winter Cabin about 160 feet away. Explore the area but please do not disturb this landmark. Technically, you take the northwesterly (rightward) Kelsey/Winter Cabin Trail to approach the cabin and spring. Behind the cabin, to the right, the spring is signed. Point the leash over a small rise beyond the sign and into the wash that is nestled among oaks, maples, grasses, and shrubs. This is an especially pretty spot in autumn, but spring snowmelt and monsoon rains afford the best chance of enjoying the spring when it is running. If there is water here, take some time for a fun splash break—purify any water you take to drink—before heading out the way you came, or make a mini-loop with Kelsey to return along the Dorsey Spring Trail (see Hike 19).

21. Parsons Spring

Round trip: 8 miles
Hiking time: 4 to 5 hours
Difficulty: easy
High point: 3852 feet
Elevation gain: 200
Best: Late September through early May
Map: Sycamore Basin USGS
Contact: Coconino National Forest, Red Rock Ranger Station (928) 282-4119
Note: Flash floods are a danger during monsoon and winter rains. Avoid this area during storms and always check weather reports before heading out. This area is now closed to camping and campfires.

Getting there: To get there from the intersection of State Hwys 260 and 89A in Cottonwood, continue on 89A (coming from Phoenix, turn left off 260). Go one mile to Historic 89A and turn north; you will pass through Old Town Cottonwood and turn east at the Tuzigoot National Monument. In 0.5 mile, you come to FR 131, also called Sycamore Canyon Road, and you take that road left (north). FR 131 is mostly unpaved and a high-clearance vehicle is recommended. Go 6.7 miles, veer left at the fork, and continue for another 3 miles to the trailhead.

This trail along Sycamore Creek is a fun and scenic amble under the cottonwood, willow, and sycamore trees that fill this desert canyon with

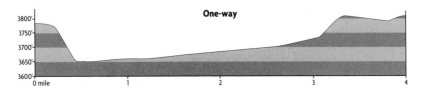

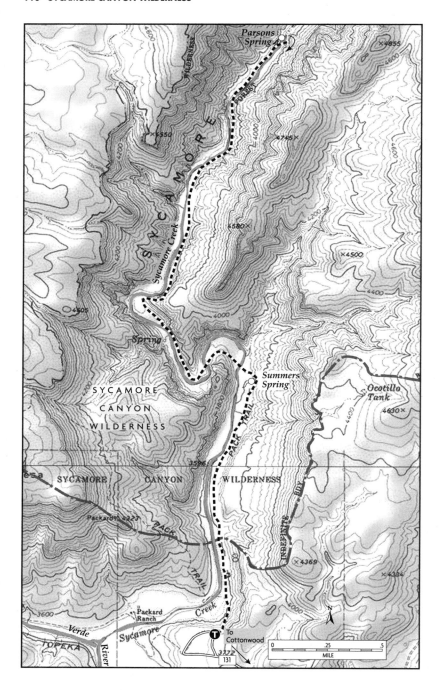

shade. In autumn, Parsons Trail is breathtaking: the pink canyon walls seem to soften against an impressionist's canopy of yellow, red, mahogany, and umber.

For hikers with dogs there is even more to love about this three-season hike: frequent stream crossings, two large pools, lots of shady cover, and a fairly soft trail over most of the route. After watering and leashing your dog, you take a steep but very short descent into the canyon. You will soon hear the rush of water—your dog will hear it first—and then see the trail fork left for Packard Trail 66 and right for Parsons Trail 144. Stay on the Parsons Trail, where the rocky, exposed canyon route ducks under the shade.

The trail immediately becomes wider and softer as you wind northward toward the creek. Sycamore Creek comes into view on your left with easy access here for a splash whenever you or your dog is ready. Of course, with five major stream crossings on this hike, there will be ample opportunity for both of you to enjoy this desert creek.

Sycamore Creek pools at the base of towering pink cliffs

The first stream crossing is at 1.75 miles. Like all the boulder hops on this hike, the trail is marked with permanent cairns so there is no guesswork involved on the opposite bank. The next stream crossing is just a shout away, at 1.8 miles. Here, the creek widens at the base of striking rose-colored bluffs. Many day hikers turn back from here but the amazing views and shady, streamside rambles will continue to reward those on a longer hike. Cross here, pick a good spot for a water and splash break for your dog, and hit the next half of the trail refreshed.

In this section, you follow the trail along the cliffs just above the creek, dipping back down creekside to cross the water at the 2.75-, 3-, and 3.5-mile marks. Large rocky beaches front the overlooks as you take to the ridges on a gentle grade. Here it is shady, there it is sunny. You have your pick on where to take in the canyon views, but just make sure that your dog gets a chance to cool off in the shady spots at least periodically in these more exposed areas.

Look closely at the grassy trailside expanses along these upper stretches of Sycamore Creek: mountain lion tracks are commonly found here, though the large cats rarely make an appearance with humans present.

As you close in on Parsons Spring, the trail descends to the creek—and shade—again and the trail becomes sandier, the air cooler. When you come to the pool at the 4-mile mark, look directly upstream; the sheer cliff before you hides the spring. Why would you turn back now? Make this crossing, take out your field glasses, and explore the spring with your dog who will enjoy the chance to cool off before hitting the exposed trail again. When you are ready, head back the way you came.

RED ROCK PHANTASMS

22. Huckaby

Round trip: 4 miles
Hiking time: 3 hours
Difficulty: easy
High point: 4550 feet
Elevation gain: 250 feet
Best: September through April
Maps: Sedona, Munds Mountain, and Munds Park USGS
Contact: Coconino National Forest, Red Rock Ranger Station, (928) 282-4119

Getting there: Getting there is simple. From Phoenix, take Interstate 17 about 100 miles north to State Hwy 179; proceed north nearly 14 miles to Sedona and turn right onto Schnebly Hill Road just before the Oak Creek bridge. (From Sedona at the intersection of Hwys 179 and 89A, head south on Hwy 179 and take a left on Schnebly Hill.) Proceed on Schnebly Hill for approximately 0.8 mile and take a left into the signed parking area. At the self-serve fee station obtain your Red Rock Ranger District day pass for $5.00 per vehicle.

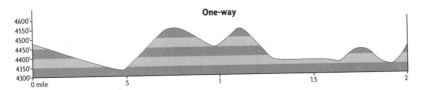

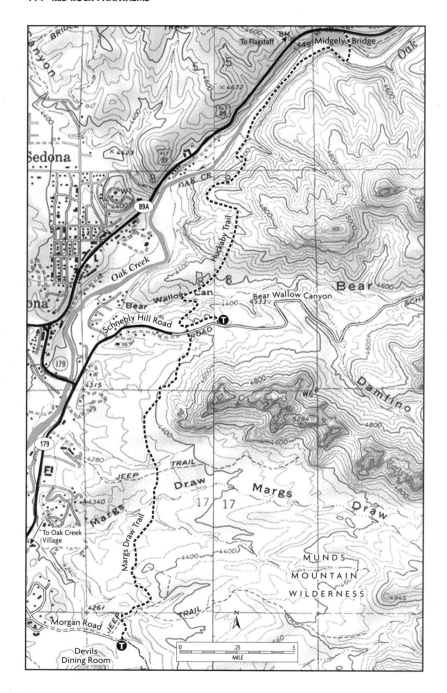

Once your dog is watered and leashed (pack in water, since access to Oak Creek is nearly 2 miles away), head left from the fee station to set out on the Huckaby Trail 161. The footpath is predominantly made up of lightly packed red dirt with occasional stretches of loose rock and a short, sandy stretch near the creek— overall, a pleasant walking surface for you and your dog. A highly scenic oak woodland landscape adorns the deep russet hills and canyons. Look for crucifixion thorn, yuccas, prickly pears, scrub oaks, agaves, manzanitas, locoweed, and fillaree, as well as junipers, Arizona cypress, sycamores, and cottonwoods. Shade is intermittent except in early morning and at creekside, so if you cannot start early plan on plenty of water breaks and let your dog soak in all the shade that is available.

A woodland dominated by pine, Arizona sycamore, and cottonwood shades your way through Oak Creek Canyon.

After rolling downhill for approximately 0.2 mile, there is a signed junction: keep straight, or west, to continue on the Huckaby Trail (the leftward fork is a segment of the Margs Draw Trail—see Hike 23). The trail climbs somewhat steeply to cross Bear Wallow Wash at 0.3 mile, reaching at 0.6 mile a beautiful vista point overlooking Bear Wallow Canyon to the east. Your heading is generally north from this point, and once you top out your climb at about the 1-mile mark, you begin paralleling Hwy 89A. Midgely Bridge, Oak Creek, Wilson Mountain, and Steamboat Rock pop into relief once you round Mitten Ridge; closer in, stunning rock formations line the trail.

At 1.5 miles, you and your dog have descended into the cool and shady riparian forest lining Oak Creek. Shortly, the trail becomes sandy, and several side paths branch off to the left offering creekside access—

use one of these if your dog is hankering for a cool dip.

At 2 miles, the cliff wall closes in on your right and directs you to a wide but safe crossing point at Oak Creek. This is a logical turnaround point, though the trail continues another 0.6 mile up another hill to the Midgely Bridge scenic overlook. When your dog has had enough of the spring-fed waters of Oak Creek, turn the leash around and go back the way you came.

23. Margs Draw

Round trip: 4 miles
Hiking time: 3 hours
Difficulty: easy
High point: 4408 feet
Elevation gain: 125 feet
Best: September through May
Maps: Sedona and Munds Mountain USGS
Contact: Coconino National Forest, Red Rock Ranger Station, (928) 282-4119
Note: The dirt access road to Broken Arrow trailhead may not be drivable by all vehicles in wet weather when the road turns to mud.

Getting there: From Phoenix, take Interstate 17 north about 100 miles to State Hwy 179; proceed north nearly 14 miles to Sedona and turn right onto Schnebly Hill Road just before the Oak Creek bridge. Go to the trailhead for Huckaby (see Hike 22) and use the self-serve fee station to obtain your Red Rock Ranger District day pass, which is $5.00 per vehicle. From Schnebly Hill take Hwy 179 South approximately 1 mile to Morgan Road. Take a left (east) toward Broken Arrow Estates and continue 0.6 miles to the end of the pavement. Just past the cattle guard there is a turnout and parking lot to your left for several spur trails.

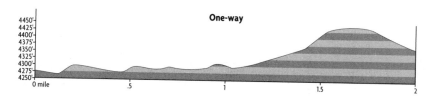

A beloved landmark: Snoopy Rock sleeps over Sedona

Margs Draw Trail 163 heads north from the entrance to the parking lot—
it is somewhat hidden among tall pinyon, juniper, and Arizona cypress
trees, but if you walk as though you are exiting the parking area, the
signed trailhead will be on your right. Once your dog is watered and
leashed (pack plenty of extra water to keep your dog's tail wagging on
this typically dry trail), you are ready to head out.

You and your dog immediately cross a wash and enter Munds Mountain Wilderness, which is open to horseback riding and hiking. You
emerge from the shaded trailhead and wash onto an exposed path—from
here, shade is intermittent but highly accessible for frequent rest and
water breaks on warmer days.

The trail leads you nearly due north over a variety of surfaces (sand,
compacted dirt, loose rocks, and slickrock), rolling in and around washes.
You start out with a gentle incline across another wash and then head
into a short (and steeper) rocky climb. In no time, you are treated with
breathtaking views of Munds Mountain to the east and north, where

Camelhead noses nearly onto the trail more than a mile away. At the 0.75-mile mark, you cut across a (usually) dry wash by traversing the top of a scenic waterfall: the terra cottas, pinks, blacks, grays, and tans of the boulders and wide, slickrock washbeds here would not be out of place in an Italian piazza.

When you round Camelhead, just past 1.25 miles, look up and to your right: the whimsical Snoopy Rock sleeps comfortably on the ridge above you. You cross several more side washes (at 1.5, 1.6, and 1.7 miles) along the way; the last offers especially scenic and shady places for a water break. You exit Munds Mountain Wilderness at 1.9 miles, just before the Schnebly Hill Road crossing. The trail terminus is less than 0.2 mile past Schnebly Hill Road, at the junction with the Huckaby Trail. Continue on to Oak Creek if you want a longer day hike (see Hike 22), or turn the leash around to return the way you came.

24. Vultee Arch

Round trip: 3.5 miles
Hiking time: 3 hours
Difficulty: easy–moderate
High point: 5235 feet
Elevation gain: 412 feet
Best: September through May
Map: Wilson Mountain USGS
Contact: Coconino National Forest, Red Rock Ranger Station, (928) 282-4119

Getting there: Accessing this trail is easy. In Sedona, from the junction of State Hwys 89A and 179, head south on 89A (through West Sedona) for 3.2 miles to the light at Dry Creek Road. Take a right, then proceed 1.9 miles to the rightward-leading Forest Road 152 just past the leftward-leading FR 152. Turn right onto FR 152 and stop at the

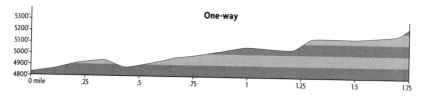

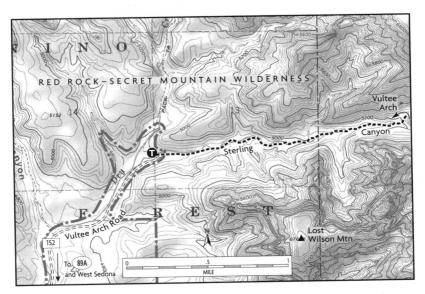

self-serve fee station; day use is $5.00 per vehicle. Proceed to the end of FR 152, which is under 5 miles; passenger cars will be fine on this maintained dirt road, but all vehicles should avoid traveling here during wet, slick mud conditions.

Two other trails spur here to the north—Bear Sign and Dry Creek; the Vultee Arch Trail 22 is to your right, running east from the trailhead. Once your dog is watered and leashed, head out—packing all the water you and your dog will need—on the narrow sandy path. This is a well-maintained and fairly well traveled trail; as such, you and your dog will likely encounter other hikers and the occasional horseback rider. Cycling is not allowed.

Within 150 feet, you cross into the Red Rock–Secret Mountain Wilderness. The path first inclines gently and is fully exposed; soon though, the yuccas, manzanitas, and prickly pears make room for shade-bearing stands of cypress, oaks, junipers, and ponderosa pines. (Ferns peek out from under boulders lining the trail, so watch that your dog does not absentmindedly graze.) Fall treats the eyes here with splashes of red in the forest canopy, while springtime offers aromatherapy: the manzanitas burst with tiny, pink-tinged bells that fairly drip with honeyed scent; nectar-logged butterflies flitting across the trail are sure to keep your dog fascinated.

Red earth, red boulders mirrored in the clear ephemeral stream along the Vultee Arch Trail

The trail to Vultee Arch leads you through the ephemeral creekbed that lines the bottom of Sterling Canyon. Red outcroppings peek through the trees on your left and Lost Wilson Mountain juts up on your right. After the 0.3-mile mark, there are numerous flat areas ideally suited for shady rest breaks. The paw-pleasing path alternates between sand, packed forest floor, and the occasional patch of easily navigated loose rocks.

At 0.75 mile, you will notice a small amount of slash and a few burn scars—signs remaining from the 1996 Arches fire. Continue east through the drainage, climbing steadily and gently, to just past the 1-mile mark with a particularly wide creekbed crossing (cairns direct you to the entry and exit points) and a stunning red rock outcropping. The path leads you and your dog through seven more crossings—after rains, this trail segment is a real doggie treat.

After your last creekbed crossing at 1.4 miles, you wind uphill to a signed junction directing you left for Vultee Arch and right for Sterling

Pass. After that left fork, the trail bends right and opens onto a gorgeous slickrock area. Save some "wows" for the view at the top, however. Follow the cairn marker toward the moderately steep (and very faint) path up and around a beautiful knob. Then make a left turn and continue to follow the cairns up to the canyon overlook.

While catching your breath and quenching your thirst, enjoy the scenic view above and to the right of the trail's namesake sandstone arch. Aviation history buffs take note. The arch is named for Gerard and Sylvia Vultee, who died nearby in an airplane crash in 1938. Gerard Vultee designed the VA1 "Lady Peace," which made the so-called Ping-Pong flight, the first round-trip flight from New York to London, in 1936. Vultee also designed a plane for newspaper mogul William Randolph Hearst. A memorial plaque in honor of Gerard and Sylvia Vultee is placed at this overlook.

The overlook is on an exposed saddle, so when your dog is ready for shade, point the leash back downhill and return the way you came.

25. Wilson Canyon

Round trip: 3 miles
Hiking time: 2.5 hours
Difficulty: easy–moderate
High point: 4887 feet
Elevation change: 443 feet
Best: September through May
Map: Munds Park USGS
Contact: Coconino National Forest, Red Rock Ranger Station,
(928) 282-4119

Getting there: To get there from the junction of Hwys 89A and 179 in Sedona, take 89A north for 1.9 miles. Cross Midgely Bridge and park in the lot on the left.

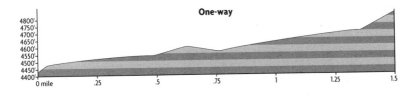

Though a well-traveled wilderness trail, the parking lot is deceptively crowded, being a launch point for several attractions: the Huckaby Trail overlook, the Midgely Bridge scenic overlook, the Wilson Mountain Trail, and the Wilson Canyon Trail 49. Horses are not recommended here and cycling is prohibited beyond the wilderness boundary, so this is effectively a hiking-only trail. Arrive early, heed the leash rules, and you and your dog will enjoy this mostly shady, cool, and very scenic hike in red rock country.

Once you have watered and leashed your dog (pack water in, as the wash is typically dry), head north from the parking lot past a picnic ramada. You will come to a signed trail junction for the Wilson Mountain and Wilson Canyon Trails—go straight ahead into Wilson Canyon. Boot and paw comfortably pad along a packed dirt path that at 0.1 mile forks right (permanent cairns direct you) and gently climbs into the canyon.

Soon, you are winding through shade cast by low-lying oaks and the cliffs on either side of the wash and trail. After winter and late-summer rains, this ephemeral creek holds a gossamer-thin veil of water for several days before the trees, lichens, grasses, and evaporation finally claim

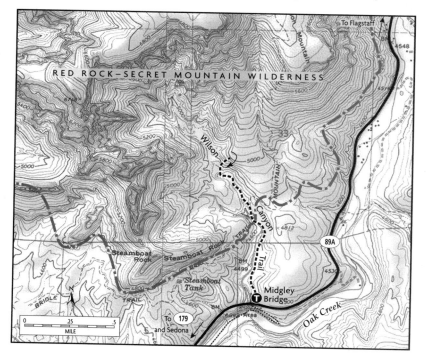

Blue after a splashy romp in Wilson Canyon

it. If you time your hike just right, your dog will enjoy frequent splashy romps from 0.4 mile on as the trail winds in and around the wash.

At 0.6 mile pass a fork leading right for another leg of the Wilson Mountain Trail and a fork leading left for the Jim Thompson Trail. At 0.7 mile, a steeper, slightly rockier ascent from the wash continues in a gentler climb up and down through the canyon—all the while facing Wilson Mountain. You are now heading northwest into the Red Rock–Secret Mountain Wilderness Area. A particularly scenic access point to the creekbed comes at 0.8 mile where you see an overhang of red bluffs: it is also an excellent, shady rest stop whether the creek is dry or running. Another easy creek crossing just before 0.9 mile through slickrock begins a short set of switchbacks uphill where you are greeted with stunning views of rock spires and the gray, tan, and rosy bands of Wilson Mountain.

Just past the 1-mile mark, you come upon a few downed trees and a short, rocky stretch of trail. This segment is fairly easy to navigate, and you are rewarded with deeper shade cover from mature cypress trees along the creekbed. As you approach 1.5 miles, the canyon narrows slightly and the trail enters the wash: prepare for wading or slick surfaces if there has been a recent rain. After a large red rock boulder outcrop on your right, scramble uphill to the saddle and enjoy dazzling views of the tree-lined canyon and mountains around you. Take in the sights before pointing the leash back the way you came.

26. Secret Mountain

Round trip: 5 miles
Hiking time: 3.5 hours
Difficulty: easy
High point: 6618 feet
Elevation change: 200 feet
Best: April through November
Maps: Loy Butte and Sycamore Point USGS
Contact: Coconino National Forest, Red Rock Ranger Station, (928) 282-4119

Getting there: From Flagstaff, take old Route 66 west for 2.6 miles, turning left onto Woody Mountain Road (you will see a sign directing you

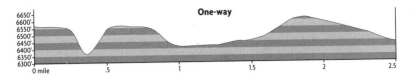

One-way

6650'
6600'
6550'
6500'
6450'
6400'
6350'
6300'
0 mile .5 1 1.5 2 2.5

to the Flagstaff Arboretum), which is also Forest Road 231. Check your odometer here. Follow FR 231 south 14 miles—13 miles of that is a well-maintained, unpaved surface, but the remaining roads require high-clearance vehicles. At the fork, take FR 538 to the right for a total of 12.3 miles. You will pass forks to Forest Roads 538E, 538D, 538A, and 538H (stay straight through these); at the fork with FR 538B, turn left to stay on FR 538, and go straight at the fork with 538K. FR 538 ends at your trailhead.

This trail into the Red Rock–Secret Mountain Wilderness is a remote and beautiful forest jaunt, open to hiking and horseback riding only. Leashes are required here, so water and leash your dog at the trailhead. Pack in plenty of water also, since this trail is typically dry in between snowmelt and rains.

Secret Mountain Trail 109 heads southeast, initially following a gentle slope downhill. The footpath is made up of a combination of surfaces, ranging from a comfortable forest floor to several loose, rocky areas on the slopes. Ponderosa pines and Gambel oaks keep you and your dog shaded and cool as you start rolling along the lip of Secret Mountain's western rim. The path zigs to the south just before a fork at 0.4 mile. Loy Canyon Trail branches to the right, but you continue straight and uphill for Secret Mountain, cresting on this climb at 0.5 mile.

A pretty ravine comes into view on your left at 0.9 mile, and you cross it shortly. The trail returns to its southerly course, leveling out after the ravine, which you follow for a time. If you are visiting in the spring or after summer rains, it is likely you will find pools in the ravine; there are pretty slickrock beaches here that offer good access for your dog to enjoy a splash break.

At 1 mile, you are climbing again and the path veers away from the ravine. Manzanitas, cacti, alligator junipers, and scrub oaks crowd the trail on this more exposed segment. Beautiful rock platforms squat on and around the trail and the path gets loose and rocky on this decline. At 1.3 mile you come to a cabin and corral tucked between the folds of two hills—water pools up in this confluence as well after snowmelt and rains. Cross the gully, pass between the corral and the cabin and head west to continue your climb. When you crest this hill, at 1.4 miles, you come to a sign directing you to turn left (southeast) for the remainder of the trail—but to the right and uphill of the sign is Secret Cabin. A faint path leads to the cabin close by, and behind it, to the west, is an overlook with the best view of the canyon bottoms found along the Secret Mountain Trail. Proceed with caution, since the drop is sheer.

Head back east to the trail junction, then take a right (south) and continue. From here, the trail is even lonelier, since many hikers turn back at this point. At 1.5 miles, you and your dog start another easy climb along meandering switchbacks. In no time, the trail rolls under shade again and levels out. You continue to wander through sunny and shady patches for the next mile, when you and Fido ascend onto a large, open ponderosa pine parkland. Fire rings are scattered about here and great picnic and water break spots abound. At the rim, there are good, if somewhat obstructed, views to the west and south of Loy Canyon, Hart Well Canyon, Casner Mountain, and beyond (on a clear day) into Sycamore Canyon. When you are ready, turn the leash back north and return the way you came.

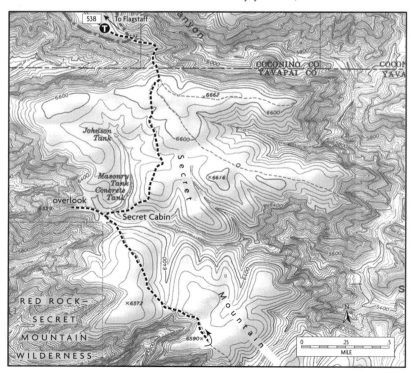

MOGOLLON RIM COUNTRY

27. Macks Crossing

Round trip: 4 miles
Hiking time: 2.5 hours
Difficulty: easy
High point: 6730 feet
Elevation change: 500 feet
Best: March through November
Maps: Quayle Hill and Leonard Canyon USGS
Contact: Coconino National Forest, Happy Jack Information Center, (928) 477-2172; or Blue Ridge Ranger Station, (928) 477-2255
Note: Given the exposure on this hike, restrict summer hikes to early morning.

Getting there: From Flagstaff, take Lake Mary Road south 54 miles to its end in Clints Well, then turn left onto State Hwy 87 heading north toward Winslow. Proceed 14 miles and take Enchanted Road (Forest Road 319) to the right; the turnoff is 0.5 mile beyond mile point 304. Turn right again in 0.2 mile onto Green Ridge Drive, which you follow for 0.5 mile, then turn right onto Juniper Drive, followed by a left onto Cedar Drive. On Cedar, you will see a sign for Forest Road 137; this is your trailhead. Park in the driveway down the hill on the right just past

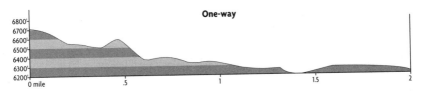

the sign so that you do not block the road. Once your dog is watered and leashed, you are ready to head down to East Clear Creek.

The trail to Macks Crossing is a short, easy hike into East Clear Creek. The creek is one of the rare, permanently flowing streams in Arizona, and you will always find water here. But since it is mostly an exposed trail, be sure to pack in water for you and your dog to have any trailside breaks you need—and as always, purify what you take to drink from the creek.

Your route follows FR 137 down to the drainage, which is rocky but not too steep. The road is closed to passenger vehicles and, though all recreational uses are allowed, the trail is a quiet, remote way into East Clear Creek. Be sure to follow the leash rule, however, because you will occasionally see ORVs on this trail.

A tree-lined cliff offers intermittent shade on your left and drops off to the right of the trail into a pretty gorge. The canyon walls are covered with pines, which makes this section feel cooler, even when you are not directly under the canopy.

At 0.5 mile you round a bend, turning east-northeast, and get your first sunlit-glints of East Clear Creek. Of course, your dog has already heard the distant sound of rushing water and soon, your human ears will catch

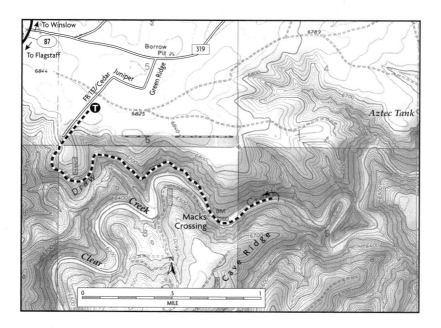

Easy access to the slow, cool waters of East Clear Creek is a real treat for your dog at the end of this exposed canyon trail.

up. About 0.2 mile before you alight onto the stream's bank, the wide, rocky roadway crumbles into a fairly hard but sandy surface—looser, sandy stretches alternate with compacted sand for the remainder of your hike. Dogs are allowed off leash at the stream, however a high concentration of bears and mountain lions in this area makes it wise to keep them under control and leashes handy.

When you reach the stream, turn left (east). At 1.4 miles, you have great access to the stream where your dog will want to cool her pads and take a dip, though it is not shady here. While your dog gets a quick, cooling dip, enjoy the twitters, flutters, buzzes, and rustles of East Clear Creek's many denizens: lizards, dragonflies, palo verde beetles, moths, butterflies, and songbirds thrive next to this lush waterway. When you are ready to find shade and continue your hike, call your soggy dog and keep padding eastward.

From here, the trail rolls away from the water, climbing up and down within the drainage; however, numerous spur trails lead to the stream. A beautiful oak grove adds a touch of fall color to the canyon just before 1.5 miles, above a group of dispersed camping sites. Columns and shelves of rock peek out from trees as you meander with your dog along the creek. Arizona cypress trees add their grace to a number of streamside groves. Watch for wide, deep pools along your way where you can join your dog for a wade or dip (it is worth the weight to pack along technical water shoes).

Your turnaround point is at 2 miles. Beyond this point, the trail is extremely faint, but it is possible to continue exploring along the creek's banks—just watch out for rattlesnakes on warmer days, especially in the thicker underbrush and among the boulders. When you are ready, point the leash back to the west and return the way you came.

28. Horse Crossing

Round trip: 3 miles
Hiking time: 2 hours
Difficulty: moderate–difficult
High point: 6956 feet
Elevation change: 544 feet
Best: April through November
Map: Blue Ridge Reservoir USGS
Contact: Coconino National Forest, Happy Jack Information Center, (928) 477-2172; or Blue Ridge Ranger Station, (928) 477-2255
Note: Forest Road 95 is closed in the winter, generally from November 15 through April 1; check with the agency to be sure the road is open before heading out.

Getting there: From Flagstaff, take Lake Mary Road south to the intersection with State Hwy 87 (54 miles). Turn north, towards Winslow, and

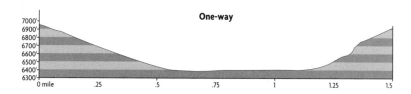

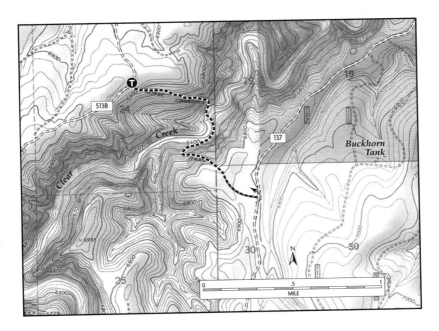

proceed 9 miles to Forest Road 95. Take FR 95 south (right) 4 miles to FR 513B and turn left. Go 2 miles to the signed trailhead. High-clearance vehicles are recommended.

Horse Crossing Trail 20, another route to East Clear Creek, provides a tougher workout than the trail at Macks Crossing (see Hike 27) but it is shadier, more remote, and open to hiking and horseback riding only. Once your dog is watered and leashed—pack in additional drinking water for the trail and treat any you take from the stream—head out onto the path from the parking circle. The trail immediately takes a sharp right and leads you and your dog south to the creek. As with nearly all rugged canyon trails that lead to water, the footpath has a few loose, rocky segments on tighter switchbacks as well as sandy stretches along the streambanks. Overall, however, the path is a paw-pleasing, compacted forest floor.

You and your dog initially follow a meandering and relatively gentle downhill route. You are padding through a mature open ponderosa pine–Gambel oak forest. Spring dresses up the parklike understory with wildflowers, while autumn splashes the sunlit oaken canopy with soft reds and salmon pinks. Ferns occasionally keep company with the lichen-covered

boulders here and there alongside the trail; see that your dog does not graze as you make your way down to the creek. Also, be alert for snakes on warmer days.

Mogollon Rim country is ruggedly beautiful, and this canyon hike does not disappoint in the view department. The jutting walls and spires above East Clear Creek peek through the forest cover throughout your trek. On the near side of the canyon, there are no switchbacks per se, but the trail doglegs occasionally to approach the creek. Pretty outcroppings and rock formations are softly illuminated by the dappled sunlight falling through the canopy. Shortly before you bottom out at 0.6 mile, you have a terrific view of the canyon walls, now rising dramatically on your left. There is a campsite, also to your left, overlooking a nook in the canyon that holds a large pool, one of many great splash spots you will find along East Clear Creek. When you are ready to continue, follow the trail southwest (to the right) and upstream. You are hiking along the creek, so your dog can splash when she needs to, but be careful not to disturb any beavers or their dams.

The trail occasionally gets vague, but you cannot miss the crossing at 0. 8 mile. The stream is split here; you can either wade or use boulders as stepping stones to get to the island. Turn right, walk in the sandy brambles of the island for a short stretch, then look across the second arm of the stream to just where it narrows and there you will see a square trail sign nailed to a ponderosa pine which directs you to the correct crossing point (0.8 mile). Turn right, heading west; once you cross the stream, the path is easy to see though overgrown with riparian shrubbery and tall grasses. At 0.9 mile, let your dog have a last splash, point the leash out of the brambles, and head out of the canyon. In just a few steps, another sign on a tree directs you to a faint footpath that veers sharply left. At 1 mile, take another left (the path is very faint here), look uphill, which is due east, and you will see the first steps for your climb.

The last half-mile of this hike is moderate to steep hiking, with tighter switchbacks and some loose, rocky segments. The trail ends at a forest road. The breathtaking views along the way are a great reward for you; your dog will get her tail wagging again after another romp in East Clear Creek when you return the way you came.

Opposite: A rugged canyon flanks the cool waters of East Clear Creek.

29. Houston Brothers to Aspen Spring

Round trip: 3 miles
Hiking time: 2 hours
Difficulty: easy
High point: 7192
Elevation gain: 110 feet
Best: April through October
Maps: Blue Ridge Reservoir and Dane Canyon USGS
Contact: Coconino National Forest, Happy Jack Information Center, (928) 477-2172; or Blue Ridge Ranger Station, (928) 477-2255

Getting there: To get there, take the Beeline Hwy (State Hwy 87) north to 9.4 miles past Clints Well. Turn right onto FR 95, a well-maintained gravel road, and continue 6.5 miles. At the East Clear Creek crossing, FR 95 heads right at a junction—take that right fork and continue on FR 95 for 4.5 miles. Pass FR 139, to turn left on FR 139A. Continue 0.2 mile to park at the Fred Haught Trail sign; the trail actually starts across the road—do not be confused by this awkwardly placed signage. Once your dog is watered and leashed, walk down the primitive road to the left of the parking area.

For Gifford Pinchot, father of the U.S. Forest Service, it was love at first sight when he visited Houston Draw. Today the towering trees, flowing springs, and rock faces staring out from the canyon make an altogether perfect setting for you and your dog to enjoy a journey back in time to Aspen Spring.

Houston Brothers Trail 171 is part of a system of trails—the Cabin Loop Trail System—linked by history as well as geography. The Forest Service built modest living quarters for firefighters on round-the-clock hazard duty during fire season; many of these cabins still stand. One such cabin,

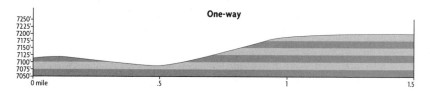

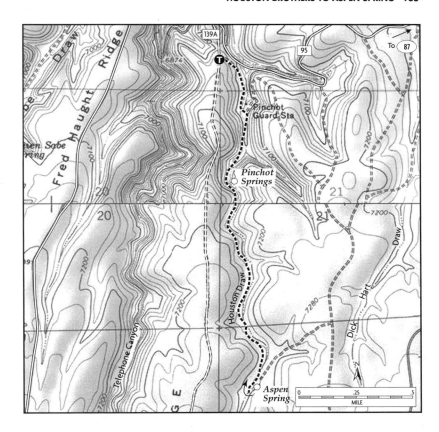

now named for Pinchot, marks the beginning of the Houston Brothers Trail, and another is within barking distance of Aspen Spring.

Just down the trail, you will spot Pinchot Cabin across a drainage and to the left of a signed trail junction. If your dog is hankering to hike, explore the cabin on your way back. From the trail junction, cross the draw and continue south along the west side of the canyon all the way to Aspen Spring.

You can set a snappy pace since the level path you are on is also soft under foot and paw. The trail offers frequent access to the draw's perennial stream if your canine friend wants a cooling dip. Should you be tempted to supplement your drinking water from the stream or springs, be sure to treat it.

You know you are in a fire-dependent forest from the aspen groves that crop up between the ponderosa pines. A particularly good time

Artemis takes an early winter sunbath on a rocky shore near Aspen Spring.

to ramble among aspens is after the first frost, usually mid-October, when their green canopy turns into a palette of golden flame—a seasonal reminder of the fires that gave them a hold on this forest in the first place.

Watch for elk moving through the parklike riparian meadows you traverse. These impressive beasts tend to travel in herds, so while on trail keep your dog on the leash as required by Forest Service rules.

Across the draw, you will notice a number of rock formations—some whimsical, some grim—that are a shutterbug's dream. Their faces change as you move along the trail, so save some film for the trip back. At 1.5 miles you come to a sign marking Aspen Spring. There is a rocky beach that makes a terrific dog launch into the shallow pool.

If your dog is still pointing her nose southward after exploring Aspen Spring, you can enjoy more of the Cabin Loop Trail System by continuing south as many as 5.5 miles. The Houston Brothers Trail links up with Barbershop and General Crook Trails. The path is tricky to find in places, and there are a few logs to navigate over or around, but watch for Forest Service blazes. The draw will keep you on the southward path toward the Mogollon Rim until you and your dog are ready to turn the leash around and head out the way you came.

30. Pivot Rock Canyon

Round trip: 3.5 miles
Hiking time: 2.5 hours
Difficulty: easy
High point: 6856 feet
Elevation change: 110 feet
Best: April through November
Maps: Pine and Calloway Butte USGS
Contact: Coconino National Forest, Happy Jack Information Center, (928) 477-2172; or Blue Ridge Ranger Station, (928) 477-2255

Getting there: From Flagstaff, take Lake Mary Road to its end at Clints Well (54 miles) and turn right (south) onto State Hwy 87. Continue past mile point 284, then turn right onto Forest Road 616 and continue approximately 3.3 miles to a campground to the right. Park here such that you do not block the road.

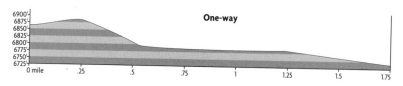

One-way

Your trailhead is at the end of the campground, about 0.25 mile in. There is no trailhead sign; you and your dog simply continue along the road, heading northwest, to take this trail (it is officially blocked to motor vehicle traffic farther up, but cycling and horseback riding are allowed in the canyon). It is a delight that Pivot Rock Creek flows much of the time, and you can often find pools of water for your dog's cooling dips. Nonetheless, be sure to water and leash your dog before setting out and pack in water for the dry spots along your way. Always treat what you drink from the stream if it is flowing.

Pivot Rock Canyon is a beautiful nook of the Mogollon Rim that is swathed in a ponderosa pine–Gambel oak–aspen forest, which means lots of cool shade for warm days and gorgeous autumn color. The footpath is largely a compacted forest floor with some short rocky sections— since the trail is so level, these stretches pose no problem for the well-conditioned dog (and hiker). Camping sites are dispersed throughout the canyon, handy for a shady water break or picnic with your pooch. One such site at 0.3 mile sits on a nice promontory overlooking the canyon and creek. Your trail veers left (west) here.

You and your dog cross the stream for the first time at 0.4 mile. On the creek's north bank is an unsigned junction, head north here (to the right). The path forks again at 0.7 mile: the road goes up to the left and a fainter trail leads to the right, toward the stream. Take the rightward path, hop down the bouldery staircase, and prepare for enchantment.

Beautiful boulders make a monolithic island in the stream, which is shallow here, with pretty pools, mossy downed logs, and improbably balanced trees clinging to the water's edge. Reflected sunlight plays against the boulders, which for all the world look (en masse) like a ship gone aground.

The path takes you to your second stream crossing—this is another hike on which technical water shoes come in handy for wading—and you and your dog emerge with the creek on your left. This is now a narrow, compacted footpath surrounded by pretty wildflowers in the spring and summer, and tucked under the shady canopy of ponderosas, oaks, and aspens. The rustle of lizards and salamanders in the tall grasses and chatter of birds will perk up your dog's ears. After two more stream crossings 1 mile into the trail, you come to another perfect break spot, should your dog like a romp, where a scenic mini-waterfall courses over boulders next to the trail.

From here, the canyon widens and you and Fido are padding through a sunnier, parklike area. You make four more stream crossings as the trail winds through the bottom of the canyon. A number of spur trails lead to some established campsites; keep heading northwest toward the junction of Pivot Rock Canyon and the Hicks and Duncan Canyon to stay on track. This hike ends at the remains of an old Civilian Conservation

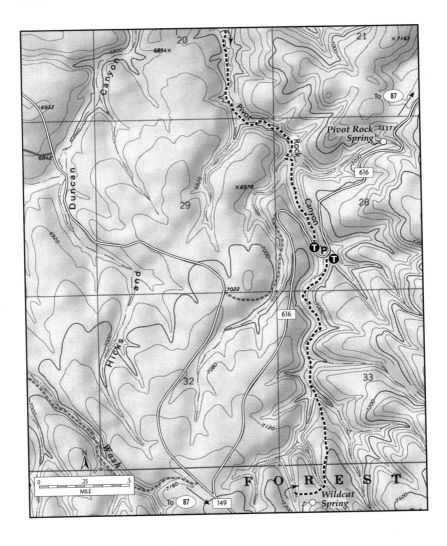

A rustic ruin nestled in the pines of Pivot Rock Canyon

Corps campground, where a log cabin, makeshift chimney, and communal cooking area still remain to the left of the trail.

When you have taken in the history of this scenic area, point the leash south and head back the way you came, allowing plenty of time for your dog to get in a few last cooling splashes on your way to the trailhead.

31. Wildcat Spring

Round trip: 3 miles
Hiking time: 2 hours
Difficulty: easy
High point: 7168 feet
Elevation change: 216 feet
Best: April through November
Maps: Pine and Calloway Butte USGS
Contact: Coconino National Forest, Happy Jack Information Center, (928) 477-2172; or Blue Ridge Ranger Station, (928) 477-2255

Getting there: From Flagstaff, take Lake Mary Road to its end at Clints Well (54 miles) and turn right (southwest) onto State Hwy 87. Just past

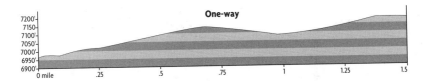

mile point 284, turn right onto Forest Road 616 and continue approximately 3.3 miles to a campground to the right. Park here such that you do not block the road. Look to the south across FR 616; you will see a "road closed" sign with a trail marker beside it. This is your trailhead.

The trail to Wildcat Spring follows Pivot Rock Canyon to the south from the same trailhead as Hike 30. Hiking, cycling, and horseback riding are allowed here, and though you should be prepared to heed trail etiquette and follow leash rules, the use of this area is still quite low. Once you have watered and leashed Fido—do not forget to pack in water, and purify what you find at the spring—you are ready to head out.

Pretty forest hikes in the hot, dry Southwest never go out of style, especially when you are traveling with your favorite canine. Tall pines, aspens, and oaks mean a harmony of greens, golds, and reds in autumn; broad, lush meadows delight the eyes in the spring when a rainbow of wildflowers shimmers on the forest floor. After snowmelt and summer rains, springs and ephemeral washes gurgle and soak the boulders and earthen banks of their surrounds.

Your footpath initially is on the left side of Pivot Rock Canyon, and parallels a creek—often flowing—on an old road. Before 0.2 mile, there is an unsigned fork. The old road you have been following goes up to the left, but you and your dog need to head downhill briefly on a fainter trail. You cross the streambed soon thereafter to continue south along the path. Pass another unsigned spur trail on the right to stay in the canyon bottoms all the way to Wildcat Spring.

The widely spaced clusters of ponderosa pines cast intermittent shade throughout your hike and the meadows offer great breaking points on your way in and out. But the real treat is the 0.5-mile segment along the streambed. Water—as always—produces astonishing lushness for such an arid region. (Ferns can be deep and high here, so see that your dog just takes in the sights.) If water is flowing, your dog will enjoy cooling her pads along this stretch, since you must cross the creek several more times. The trail is faint after the last stream crossing—at 0.7 mile—

continue about 25 yards to pick up an old road, heading south, a comfortable walking surface, with just a few loose rocks here and there amid the duff.

At 1.2 miles, just 0.2 mile before the spring, the road turns west and you peer into a side canyon just ahead. Your goal, Wildcat Spring—now channeled into a concrete catchment—is signed and easy to find uphill and to the left of the path. (Like most ephemeral springs in the southwest, this one is typically dry.) You can explore more here, since the road continues a bit further, or take a shady play break with your dog before pointing the leash east and heading out the way you came.

32. Calloway

Round trip: 1.5 miles
Hiking time: 2 hours
Difficulty: moderate–difficult
High point: 6348 feet
Elevation gain: 600 feet
Best: April through November
Map: Calloway Butte USGS
Contact: Coconino National Forest, Happy Jack Information Center, (928) 477-2172; or Blue Ridge Ranger Station, (928) 477-2255
Note: Watch summertime temperatures and go early if temperature is suitable.

Getting there: From Flagstaff, take Lake Mary Road to its junction with State Hwy 87 (54 miles). Take 87 southwest (right) for 12 miles to Hwy 260. Turn north (right) and follow Hwy 260 to mile point 249; take a right onto Forest Road 144, not signed from the road, but you do see a sign when you turn. Check your odometer here. The road forks at 1.8 miles; follow the sign to turn left on FR 149. Take FR 149 for 1.25 miles to FR 142, and in 2.8 miles, turn right onto FR 142B. There is no sign, but a large snag with a red spray-painted "B" on it. You come to the trailhead in 2.4 miles. This is a very rough road that requires high-clearance vehicles.

Opposite: Pretty forest meadows make great romp and rest grounds for you and your dog on your way to Wildcat Spring.

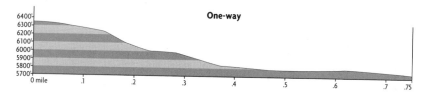

Once your dog is watered and leashed, head east from the parking lot through a fence opening. Within 50 steps, you have crossed into the West Clear Creek Wilderness Area and onto the brink of a lovely, remote canyon with a gorgeous view into the canyon before you. And since this is a short hike, you seem to plunge, rather than walk, to the creekside. Calloway Trail 33 briefly ducks under the cover of a mixed pine and oak forest—transitioning to a pinyon-juniper ecosystem as it loses elevation—and your demanding drop into the canyon is made

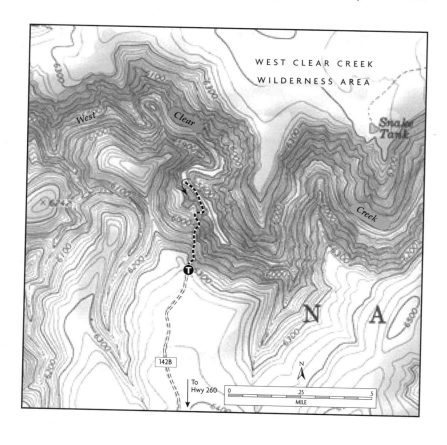

Rugged outcrops house equally rugged—and beautiful—flora above West Clear Creek.

quite pleasant with the shade and promise of water from this perennial creek below.

Though there is generally a very comfortable trail surface of compacted forest floor, there are several loose and rocky sections, so take the tight switchbacks with care and wear good footgear with ankle support. It is worth the weight in your pack to bring along some technical sandals so that you can safely navigate the slickrock bottoms of West Clear Creek. And speaking of the creek, you can hear the sound of rushing water along your entire hike—sure to keep your dog's tail wagging all the way down.

At streamside (just under 0.75 mile) there are some terrific rest spots—some shady, some sunny—and endless exploring to be done by wading or boulder-hopping. Autumn color glitzes up the desert and evergreen foliage that clings to the canyon walls, but West Clear Creek is always a showy setting with playful dances of light and dive-bombing dragonflies to catch your eye and your dog's fancy.

There is a 0.2-mile stretch—almost directly in the middle of this moderately steep trail—with only patchy shade, so be sure to give your dog plenty of time for a cooling dip before heading out the way you came.

33. Maxwell

Round trip: 1.7 miles
Hiking time: 2 hours
Difficulty: moderate–difficult
High point: 6729 feet
Elevation change: 729 feet
Best: April through November
Map: Calloway Butte USGS
Contact: Coconino National Forest, Happy Jack Information Center, (928) 477-2172; or Blue Ridge Ranger Station, (928) 477-2255
Note: Watch summertime temperatures and go early if temperature is suitable.

Getting there: From Flagstaff, take Lake Mary Road for 46.5 miles, past mile point 297, and turn right onto Forest Road 81 (high clearance is needed for the more remote backcountry roads here). In 3.1 miles, the

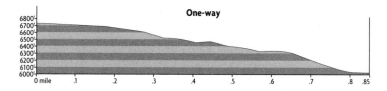

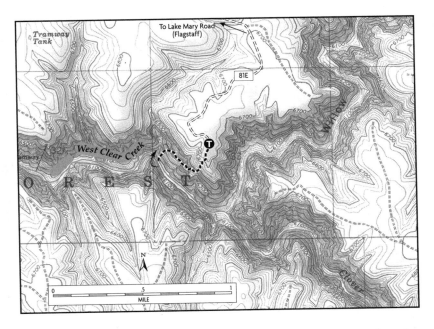

road forks and you head left onto FR 81E. Drive 3.8 miles and at the next fork, stay left on 81E for 2 miles. The road ends at a primitive campground; take a left onto the unmarked road and proceed 0.25 mile. You will see a parking area to your right, signed with an unnumbered Forest Service stake. From the parking area, walk east and downhill and you will see the registration podium; this is your trailhead.

Maxwell Trail 37 offers a similar experience to Hike 32 but a much easier drive to the trailhead. Once your dog is watered and leashed (pack in water since the hike to and from the creek is strenuous; you will need to purify what you take to drink from the stream), head downhill along what is initially a compacted forest floor. Unlike the Calloway Trail, this trail starts in the shade of parklike stands of ponderosa pines at the canyon's top. Given the steepness of this hike, the surface is terrific—some loose gravel and rocks pop up only occasionally along a footpath composed of sturdy boulders and compacted forest floor.

Spring and autumn are the showiest seasons along the Maxwell Trail when wildflowers and oaks dress up the canyon walls and canopy; but the appeal of cool, splashy romps in our hot Arizona summer is irresistible. And in any season, this pink-tinged canyon is generous with views both

Striking rock forms line the canyon walls in the West Clear Creek Wilderness.

at distance and close in. The first vista opens up at 0.1 as you emerge from the shade: across the canyon are jumbled layers of rock that look as though they were thrown into a basket and shaken gently until settled. In a few short steps, you and your dog happen upon a jutting promontory that offers more long-distance views and overlooks the swoops and swerves of the trail down to the creek.

In no time at all, you arrive on the banks of West Clear Creek. There is some spotty shade and no official trail here. Use-paths can sometimes be detected, but due to changing water levels—and permanent streamflow—these are unreliable. Your best bet is to explore on durable surfaces or to wade in the water. Be on the lookout for both snakes and poison ivy. Bring along technical water shoes to make the wading more fun and safe, and to make your hike out less sloshy—short as this hike is, you will need dry shoes and socks to handle the steeper segments and avoid blisters.

When your dog has had her romp and you have explored what you like of these remote and wild waters, point the leash uphill and head out the way you came.

34. Fossil Springs

Round trip: 8 miles
Hiking time: 5 hours
Difficulty: moderate–difficult
High point: 5670 feet
Elevation change: 1360
Best: late September through early May
Map: Strawberry USGS
Contact: Coconino National Forest, Red Rock Ranger Station, (928) 282-4119
Note: Flash floods pose a danger—avoid this trail during monsoon or winter storm. The trailhead is located in the Tonto National Forest; during fire season and after winter snows, contact the Payson Ranger Station for fire restrictions or road conditions at (926) 474-4900.

Getting there: From Flagstaff, take Lake Mary Road south for 54 miles to its end at Clints Well and turn southwest (right). Proceed 19.7 miles to Strawberry and take a right (west) onto Fossil Creek Road, also known as Forest Road 708. Follow FR 708 five miles, take the signed turnoff right and proceed less than one mile to the parking circle (and your trailhead).

The Fossil Springs Wilderness Area—open to hiking and horseback riding only—is a small wilderness along the Mogollon Rim north of the Mazatzals. By January 2005, the dam above Fossil Creek will be decommissioned, meaning that this area will be that much wilder—and more watery—good news for the abundant avian wildlife, javelinas, mountain lions, riparian flora, and recreationists who enjoy seeking out rare perennial desert waters. Current campsites and access trails to the creek will be reconfigured or relocated altogether over time. Contact the Ranger

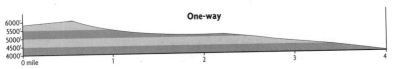

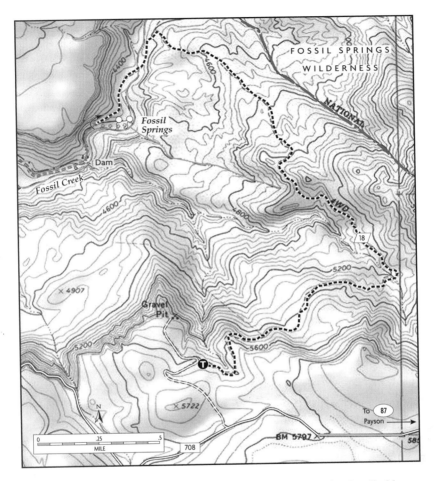

Station if you plan to extend your trip beyond the day hike detailed here.

Once at the trailhead for Fossil Springs Trail 18, water and leash your dog. Be sure to pack in more water—your destination is a sprawling, lush oasis along Fossil Creek, but the way there is a largely open trail in a pinyon-juniper ecosystem. During winter, also bring a lightweight pack towel and your dog's vest to protect her from hypothermia after she enjoys some splash time in the creek. A sign at the trailhead directs you left onto an old road with a comfortable gravel surface initially heading northwest. The trail forks in less than 0.1 mile; take a right to head downhill and

Opposite: Springs and seeps feed the cool, mineral-rich waters of Fossil Creek.

take a right again onto the road, heading northeast. Once on the road again, the grade is gentle and the views of Hardscrabble Mesa and the canyons beyond are dramatic. Hills and crags are mottled and banded with reds, beiges, grays, and pinks and, in the distance, the covering vegetation looks deceptively smooth.

For nearly the first 3 miles, you and your dog will enjoy only intermittent shade from the junipers, pinyons, Gambel oaks, and velvet ash trees that pop up along the side of the trail. Fall color is beautiful here, especially creekside. The vegetation along your descent is characterized by evergreens and high desert community plants, such as scrub oak, agaves, yuccas, and in wet years, delicate wildflowers.

You cover significant elevation change on this hike, and the initially gentle grade of the old roadway is deceptive. After 0.5 mile, the trail narrows somewhat and alternates between gentle declines and moderately steep drops: here the path is comfortable gravel or packed dirt, there it is loose and rocky. Wear sturdy footgear (bring along technical sandals for wading) and take your time—on warm days, make sure your hardworking trail dog has plenty of splash time in the creek and plan to break often in the shade on your way out.

Glorious views greet you as you round a corner at 1.8 miles. A perfect, halfway rest point for the way back is at 2.1 miles in a beautiful, tree-lined clearing followed by, at 2.75 miles, a postcard view with rippling canyons. Your path is a sun-bleached terra-cotta now, comfortable under boot and paw.

At 3 miles, you come to the Fossil Creek Wilderness Boundary; go through the Z-gate and continue downhill; just shy of 3.25 miles you come to a trail junction sign directing you left for Fossil Springs and right for the Mail Trail. On your west-southwesterly route to Fossil Springs, you are now following the creek's drainage on a mostly level, and narrower, path.

At just past 3.3 miles, you cross Fossil Creek on stepping stones or by wading; proceed with caution and turn left onto the bouldery north bank. Be alert for snakes here—keep Fido on her leash, following the rules, and watch where her curious nose wants to go. Before long, you and your dog duck into a moist, cool, and green twilight world, thanks to the thick canopy of cottonwood, Arizona sycamore, and nearly thirty other species of trees in the wilderness around you. The trail is all but obscured by a carpet of blackberry bushes. Springs are plentiful (treat any water you take), and many side paths take you to the creekside, with slickrock or earthen beaches offering plenty of nooks for you and your dog to wade or swim before turning around to return the way you came in—if you can bear to leave these cool, sapphire waters.

35. Deadman Mesa

Round trip: 8.2 to 9.2 miles
Hiking time: 5 to 6 hours
Difficulty: difficult
High point: 4485 feet
Elevation gain: 1814 feet
Best: October through April
Map: Verde Hot Springs USGS
Contact: Tonto National Forest, Payson Ranger Station, (928) 474-7900

Getting there: From Flagstaff, take Lake Mary Road south for 54 miles to its end at Clints Well and turn southwest (right). Proceed 19.7 miles to Strawberry and take a right (west) onto Fossil Creek Road, also known as Forest Road 708. Follow FR 708 for 5 miles and take a left (south) onto FR 591. Proceed on this four-wheel-drive road 6.4 miles and through four gates, the last of which has a sign marking Trail 17 (the Deadman Mesa Trail), until you come to the trailhead.

You and your dog are on your way to a scenic and a dizzying drop into the Verde River basin and the northern reaches of the Mazatzal Wilderness Area. Pack in water for the hike and plan to filter any that you take from Fossil Creek. Leashes are optional beyond the trailhead here, as long as your dog responds to voice control. Voice control for your dog is crucial here, since the climb would be difficult if attempting to manage your dog on a lead. Once you and your dog are ready, head south along Deadman Mesa from the trailhead. Your path is fairly soft on boot and paw initially, with sporadic shade from the clusters of pinyon pines and squat junipers that dominate the landscape here. Some

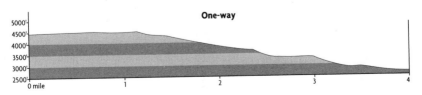

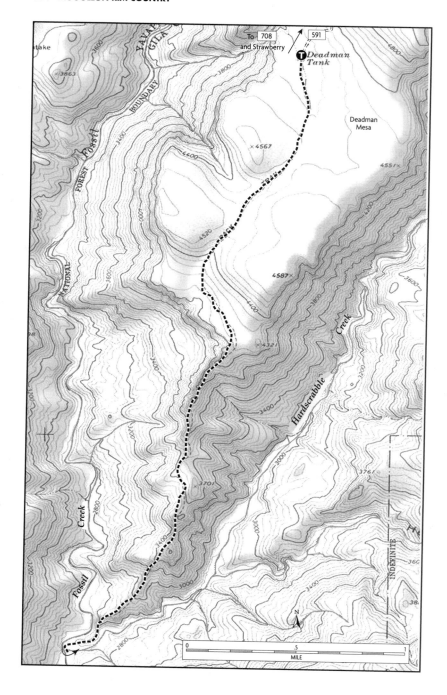

Looking into the northern Mazatzal Mountains from Deadman Mesa

prickly pear and mammalaria cacti occasionally encroach upon the foot-path so keep your dog close. Make sure she stays on the trail, and have your cactus comb handy.

The route that you and your dog are following is an old pack trail. Use is light and the path occasionally fades along this first stretch, so watch for cairns to guide you. You follow a slight incline at 0.5 mile, then the path levels out again as it winds toward the edge of the mesa. There is a very pretty, arborous grotto at 0.9 mile where the rocks form a small basin that holds water after rains. Another good rest spot is a shady grove at 1.4 miles. Take time to enjoy these respites from your exposed trail, especially on the way out, when you will have just completed a rough climb.

You are losing elevation now, approaching a ridgeline that will take you a large part of the way down to the banks of Fossil Creek. Barrel cacti and crucifixion thorn line the trail, and your dog's heightened senses will probably alert you to a variety of lizards, centipedes, and beetles making their progress alongside you. At 1.5 miles, a stunning view opens up to your right of the mesa's crinkly vertical folds. Soon you go through the ruins of a gate and begin switching down into the canyon from a gnarled finger on the mesa that is pointing south. This begins your rocky and steep descent into the Mazatzal Wilderness. Footing is tricky in places and the drop to your left is sheer, so this hike should be reserved for conditioned, experienced trail dogs and hikers.

For you the downhill vault offers terrific bird's-eye views of a scenic river valley, and for your dog the reward is little more than a mile away, when you approach Fossil Creek. Fossil Creek runs perennially, and a saunter along its banks almost to the confluence of the Verde River is well worth your significant effort. Along the last 1.25 miles of the hike, you and your dog will enjoy a relatively level stretch of Fossil Creek, where there are limitless possibilities for shade, splash, and treat breaks. The trail frequently gets washed out here as the watercourse changes with seasonal rains. If the path disappears, simply stick to the shady creek banks. Keep on the lookout for snakes. Continue southward—consulting your topographical map and GPS if necessary—and you will find the official trail. At approximately 3.75 miles, the trail zigs southeast away from the banks of Fossil Creek to pick up the Verde Trail 11, which is your turnaround point.

If your dog is still enjoying her romp time in the river valley, extend your hike 0.5 mile (one way) south along the Verde Trail to take a splash in one of America's designated "Wild and Scenic Rivers" before turning uphill and heading back the way you came.

36. Red Rock Spring

Round trip: 2 miles
Hiking time: 1.5 hours
Difficulty: easy
High point: 6000 feet
Elevation gain: 600 feet
Best: September through November, March through May
Map: Buckhead Mesa USGS
Contact: Tonto National Forest, Payson Ranger Station, (928) 474-7900

Getting there: To get there from Payson, go north for about 12 miles on the Beeline Hwy (State Hwy 87) and turn east (right) at Control Road, which is Forest Road 64. Proceed for 2.4 miles, approximately 0.8 mile beyond the sign marking Shannon Gulch. You will see a small sign for Forest Road 294 on your left—turn and park in the lot immediately before you.

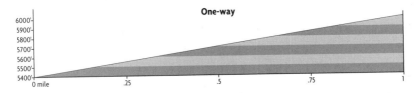

Once your dog is watered and leashed—pack in additional water in case the spring is dry—head up the path beyond the barricade. On Trail 294 you are padding along an old logging road that leads northwest directly to Red Rock Spring. Under boot and paw, the road is a pleasing combination of dirt and gravel. The canopy is a lush jumble of fairly young but tall ponderosa pines, oaks, and junipers, including the scaly alligator subspecies; at your dog's eye level, manzanitas, agaves, and boulders cling to the forest floor. Your walk is shaded and the climb is gentle and steady through this palette of reds and greens tucked under the Mogollon Rim.

At just under a mile, you will see a sign directing you to Red Rock Spring by turning right and heading a short way along the Highline Trail. The area is lush—the best indication of water even when the spring is not flowing—the shade is inviting, and your views of the rocky red bluffs to the east are magnificent.

Red Rock Spring has been a watering hole for area travelers and

Zane Grey country: A view from the Red Rock Spring Trail

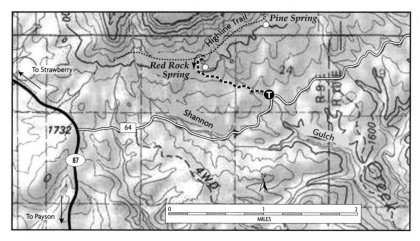

nearby residents for countless years. Apaches and pioneers alike often relied on its waters while traversing these forest byways. Eventually, in the 1870s, the Highline Trail emerged as a route connecting various homesteads in the region, and a century later it became part of the National Recreation Trail system. This is also Zane Grey country—the famous western genre novelist had a cabin right along the trail and wrote a number of his books here.

If the bluffs call and the tail is still wagging, explore the Highline Trail further: from Red Rock Spring, continue northeast and enjoy Pine Spring, only one mile away. Head back the way you came when you are ready.

37. Horton Creek

Round trip: 8 miles
Hiking time: 4 hours
Difficulty: moderate
High point: 6687 feet
Elevation gain: 1207 feet
Best: March through November
Map: Promontory Butte USGS
Contact: Tonto National Forest, Payson Ranger Station, (928) 474-7900

Getting there: From the Phoenix area, take Shea Boulevard to the Beeline Hwy (State Hwy 87) and proceed northeast to Payson. In Payson,

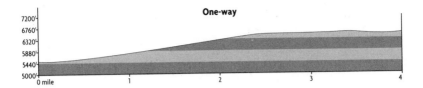

One-way

turn east onto Arizona 260. In approximately 17 miles, you will come to Kohls Ranch—take the first left after you pass the ranch to turn into the Upper Tonto Creek Campground. The trailhead is in the campground, just up the hill from the campground's gate. Park in the Horton picnic area across the creek.

Want a cool summer hike? Take your dog to Horton Creek and enjoy a splash or three between gentle climbs up this scenic Mogollon Rim trail.

The wide, level path that greets you at the trailhead for Horton Creek Trail 285 meanders briefly through an open meadow, then climbs steadily into a mixed forest of old-growth ponderosa pines, Gambel oak, Arizona sycamores, and the scaly barked alligator juniper. (For courtesy's sake, resist the urge to skirt the leash rules—during summer months, this can be a busy trail.) From here, enjoy the gurgling creek, blushing Rim-country cliffs, and towering trees along the trail.

Once you have passed through the second Forest Service gate at the 0.5-mile mark, you enter the forest canopy and take a steady northeasterly path—except where there are wide switchbacks—the entire way. The path generally is a packed forest floor, softened by pine duff and leaf litter, which becomes narrow and grassy in places. This is easier on your dog's pads than the rocky switchbacks towards the middle and end of the hike—be sure to have your dog's booties handy in case of injuries or if her pads are not fully conditioned yet.

At the 1.5-mile mark, there is one of many short side trails that take you down to the creek—it is best to use these established access points rather than blaze new trails. In 2.75 miles, the trail forks as you are climbing a ridge; the rocky path uphill to your left is the trail—a cairn marks the rightward path that leads down a steep side trail to a pretty waterfall. *Note: The water here is fairly swift and deep and the banks are narrow and slippery from the spray—you must exercise extreme caution if you approach the streamside here.* After you have feasted your eyes on the falls, you can double back to give your dog some playtime in shallower waters before heading up this side trail back to the path up to Horton

On a shady forest path to Horton Spring

Spring. In all, you have only added 0.4 mile to your hike by visiting the falls.

At the 4-mile mark, Horton Spring sputters from the Rim, flowing fairly heavily in wet years. This is an ideal play and rest area for you and your dog. Should you like to explore the area further, there is a junction for the Highline Trail, or save it for another sweltering summer day and head out the way you came.

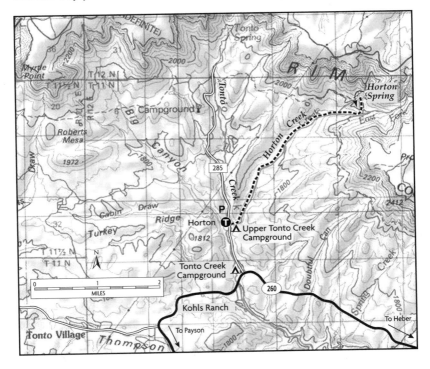

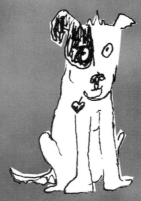

Central and Western Arizona

MAZATZAL MOUNTAINS AND AREA

38. Four Peaks Loop

Round trip: 4 miles
Hiking time: 3 hours
Difficulty: moderate–difficult
High point: 6800 feet
Elevation gain: 1160 feet
Best: late September through late April
Map: Four Peaks USGS Map
Contact: Tonto National Forest, Mesa Ranger Station, (480) 610-3300

Getting there: From the Phoenix area, take Shea Boulevard to the Bee-line Hwy (State Hwy 87) and head northeast toward Payson for 20 miles. At Four Peaks Road (Forest Road 143), take a right. The next 19 miles require a high clearance vehicle. At the Brushy Basin/Cotton-wood Camp sign, take the left fork. Continue on FR 143 about 4 miles; you will again veer left at a fork. At 18 miles, turn right on FR 648 where you will see a sign for Lone Pine trailhead. FR 648 ends in 1 mile at the trailhead.

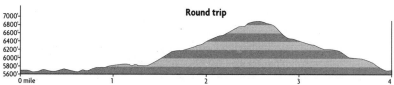

This loop offers scenic beauty, shade, and excellent three-season hiking, including winter snow trekking. (In fact, fans of winter hiking who have dogs that enjoy bounding through snow should plan to bring step-in

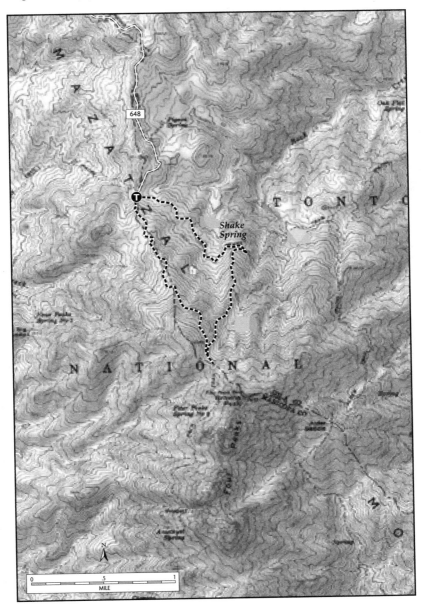

A pretty forest path holds onto winter.

crampons for traversing the steeper segments at higher elevations on this hike.) Once your dog is watered and leashed—pack in the water you will need—head onto Four Peaks Trail 130, which is a left turn from the trailhead. Your loop runs clockwise and initially southeast. Almost immediately, you cross into Four Peaks Wilderness Area, a pristine, if well-traveled, pinyon-juniper-oak woodland south of the Mazatzal Mountains. The trail itself is a combination of paw-pleasing gravel and packed forest floor.

Though the first two-thirds of this loop gains more than 1000 feet of elevation, you begin with a gentle and shady descent through alligator junipers, pinyons, and oaks. But before 0.25 mile, your climb begins and is rewarded early on with views to the east of Roosevelt Lake's turquoise waters and sneak-peeks through the trees at the distinctive crags of Brown's Peak. At 0.6 mile, you have approximately 1.5 miles ahead of you with nearly full exposure—be sure to take this into account when planning water breaks.

Just before 0.75 mile, you begin to see signs of the 1996 Lone fire and pass amid charred fallen branches and tree boles. The trail is easy to pick up by heading along the ridgeline to your left and keeping to your easterly route.

At just over 1 mile, you arrive at the signed Amethyst Trail 253 junction, and it is time for a fast zoom on Brown's Peak as your climb intensifies. Fortunately, there are some welcome shady spots at the beginning of the Amethyst Trail from towering trees and shade from the peaks during parts of the day.

Winter hiking here is spectacular because only parts of these trails keep snow on the ground for any length of time. Dogs love the slushy snow, but the slush can also turn to ice. You will want to bring crampons because this is a hike that touches the bottom of the snowfall range for Arizona, and the snow-melt-freeze cycle can produce icy patches on the trail. Check your dog's pads occasionally to see that she is not collecting painful clumps of snow and grit between her toes. Watch her for signs of hypothermia and put on her vest to keep her warm along shadier stretches.

At 1.5 miles, a particularly stunning side of Brown's Peak comes into view. The mountaintop keeps you company all the way until the Brown's Trail 133 junction, where you take a right and head downhill.

Here again, you see signs of the Lone fire. In a typical mosaic burn, the fire skipped over some areas, leaving patches of trees behind, but shrubs dominate this landscape for now. As the wind rises, listen to burned tree branches that act like bows and strings, filling the air with odd squeaks and groans.

As you wind around to the north and northeast on the Brown's Trail, lovely rock formations close in on your path. Past the 2.5 mile mark, you pass an unsigned trail junction—continue downhill and to your right to stay on the Brown's Trail. You have descended below the burned area and are again walking through a pristine woodland that will shade the rest of your hike. Several excellent rest break and picnicking spots cluster around the 3.5-mile mark, tucked in and among the boulders. Take time for you and your dog to relax in the shade before continuing the last 0.5 mile of this woodland loop to the trailhead.

39. Little Saddle Mountain

Round trip: 8 miles
Hiking time: 4 hours
Difficulty: moderate–difficult
High point: 5020 feet
Elevation gain: 1300 feet
Best: September through April
Map: Reno Pass USGS
Contact: Tonto National Forest, Mesa Ranger Station, (480) 610-3300

Getting there: From the Phoenix area, take Shea Boulevard to the Bee-line Hwy (State Hwy 87), from here proceed about 30 miles northeast toward Payson. Just past milepost 222, you will turn left at the Sycamore Creek turnoff, which is the old Hwy 87. Continue to the 3.4-mile mark. On your way, you will see two sets of large power lines that slant across the road. On your left about 100 yards beyond the second set of power lines is a large metal Arizona Trail sign, which marks a small horseshoe-shaped parking area. The Cross F trailhead is across the road (on the west side) about 20 feet before the parking lot turnoff, back towards the power lines. No Mutt Mitts are available, so bring bags to pack out your dog's waste.

The northeastern range of the Mazatzal Mountains makes up a remote and little-traveled wilderness area that offers outstanding day- and backpacking trips with high scenic value. Your dog will especially love being at heel for this trail, with its frequent shady washes and ephemeral streams. (Due to recent fires, some shade is lost, so plan to go during cooler times of day and heed the season suggestion.) Take care to pack in water for this hike, since water sources are not reliable except in rainy seasons.

Once paw and boot hit the trail, you begin rolling up the hills. Proceed through two Forest Service gates and close them after you. A cairn marks the rightward path for Little Saddle Mountain Trail and you and your dog make a moderate climb on this exposed and rocky trail. At 0.5 mile, a sign marks the junction for Little Saddle Mountain Trail 244, Cross F trailhead, and Sunflower Trail. Continue on the upward, rightward path.

You go through another gate at 0.6 mile marking the Mazatzal Wilderness boundary and signifying that this trail is part of the Arizona Trail system. You start seeing some of what the fuss is about with this area—scenic views open up and beautiful rock formations line the trail. Keep checking the ground before you, however. This area shows signs of grazing disturbance (some limited grazing is still allowed here) mainly in the form of occasionally dense prickly pear stands. Keep your dog's nose and paws well away from pads that have fallen onto the trail.

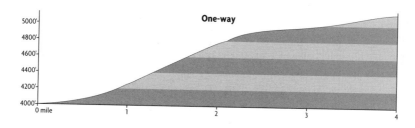

Ken and Sparky head for shade along the Little Saddle Mountain Trail.

At 0.8 mile, you make a series of moderate rises and descents as you wind into a drainage that takes the trail north and west. Your first stream (or wash) crossing is at the 1.3-mile mark. Very shortly, cairns mark five

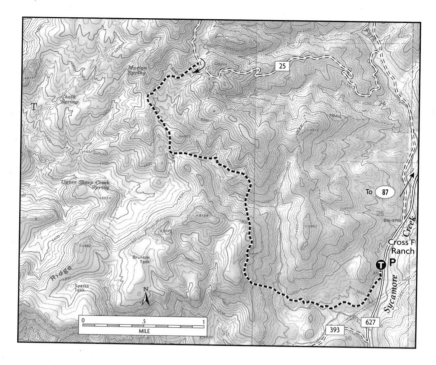

more stream crossings. After the last one, at just under 2 miles, you see an Arizona Trail sign and then an unmarked stream crossing just beyond that. Shortly thereafter, yet another stream crossing—this one has no cairns or signage but the trail is easy to pick up.

Here, you exit the creek bottom and climb on exposed terrain for nearly 0.7 mile. The path rolls down into cottonwood and sycamore studded creekbeds again—welcome shade and seasonal water (or at least a water break) cool you and your dog off, readying you both for a rewarding ascent to the 3 mile mark.

On this incline, the trail heads west, crossing a ridge. Let your eyes wander toward the southwest to catch a glimpse of Pinnacle Peak and you might catch the steady glide of a golden eagle.

After you and your dog follow a northward turn in the trail, you will make one last steep ascent for 0.25 mile. Then, the last section of the Little Saddle Mountain Trail heads northeast and follows an old jeep trail to the Saddle Mountain Trail junction at 4 miles. Explore this area after you size up your water supply, and return the way you came when you are ready to enjoy a downhill jaunt.

40. Cave Creek

Round trip: 10 miles
Hiking time: 5 to 6 hours
Difficulty: moderate
High point: 3440 feet
Elevation change: 840 feet
Best: September through May
Map: Cave Creek USGS
Contact: Tonto National Forest, Cave Creek Ranger Station,
(480) 595-3300
Note: Avoid during rains; check with the agency for trail and road conditions during rainy season.

Getting there: From Phoenix, take Cave Creek Road past the towns of Cave Creek and Carefree (about 20 miles) until it turns into Forest Road 24 which is also called Seven Springs Road. Continue north on FR 24 for 12 miles; this is a good dirt road but high-clearance vehicles are recommended due to wash overflows you encounter along the way. You will go through the Seven Springs Recreation area past a historic but still operating Civilian Conservation Corps campground. (A $4.00 day use fee is required for this area, and a drive-through fee station is available just before the recreation area.) Cross Seven Springs Wash and park at the Cave Creek trailhead parking area on the left.

Permanent streams are an oddity in the desert Southwest. It's a good thing for you and your trail dog that the Tonto National Forest has developed the Cave Creek Trail system, which in addition to Cave Creek Trail 4 includes the Skunk Tank, Cottonwood, Skull Mesa, and Quien Sabe Trails.

Start exploring this unique and beautiful area with the Cave Creek Trail. You and your dog will be walking in the footsteps of the Hohokam and Tonto Apache peoples, who at different times used this lush riparian area

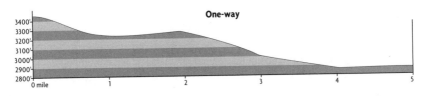

extensively. Little wonder. This thriving creek flows even in dry cycles and offers plenty of shady stretches among mighty cottonwoods and sycamores with easy access to the stream.

Once you have watered and leashed your dog, start hiking on the trail above the campground. Have you packed some spare bags? It's important to pick up after your dog in fragile desert environments. This first 0.5 mile is an exposed path on a ridge. You will cross a side road and pick up the path that quickly ducks under the shade of cottonwood and sycamore trees that thrive in the creek's watershed. Soon, your dog's sense of smell and hearing kick in and she will let you know that the creek is flowing off to your left. It will not take long for your own senses to pick up on the slight shift in humidity that desert dwellers live for on hikes like this.

Go through a Forest Service gate at the 1.2-mile mark and continue following the creek through the shady path. On this part of the trail, there are limitless access points for your dog to take a shallow dip.

At 2 miles, the trail appears to dead-end at the creekside, but if you spy the ridge across the water, you will see a path. Except during rainy seasons (when you should avoid this trail), this is an easy creek crossing. Your dog will appreciate this time to splash around now because it is here that the trail departs from the streamside and begins the first of several forays onto the ridges above the creek. Though the overall elevation gain is modest on this hike, the path wanders to and from the stream—gaining and losing elevation—many times.

At 3 miles, there is an especially wide creek crossing and an island in the creek. The trail beyond the creek is marked with a Forest Service trail sign— you cannot lose your way. The next 2 miles take you and your dog up and

Butterflies and bees sup on jimmyweed along the Cave Creek Trail.

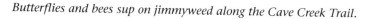

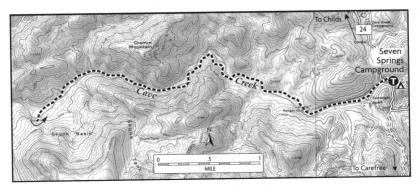

back to the creek from the canyon ridges. Above the creek, the vegetation is more typical of the Sonoran Desert than the riparian habitat you are exploring. Cacti, acacia, and even the rare Arizona agave dot the landscape.

Another major stream crossing at the 5-mile mark is next to a gentle bend in the creek and a clearing suitable for a break. (You can continue all the way to Spur Cross Road, another 5 miles, on this trail; be aware that that segment is more exposed, so carry in plenty of water or purify water from the creek.) After rest and playtime, you and your dog might want to slow your pace on the return trip to seek out the prolific rock art, or petroglyphs, and Native American ruins that are scattered throughout the streamside areas.

41. Verde River from Sheep Bridge

Round trip: 4 miles
Hiking time: 3 hours
Difficulty: easy
High point: 2424 feet
Elevation change: 344 feet
Best: October through April
Map: Chalk Mountain USGS
Contact: Tonto National Forest, Cave Creek Ranger Station, (928) 595-3300

Getting there: From Phoenix take Cave Creek Road about 20 miles to Carefree, where it turns into Forest Road 24. Continue on FR 24 through the Seven Springs Recreation Area (you are not required to pay a fee for this hike); stay on FR 24 until it ends and take a right onto FR 269 for 12 miles to Sheep Bridge. When FR 269 forks, continue forward to get to the bridge; at the bridge, there is a small lot where you can park off-road.

Please remember to bring bags to use to pick up after your dog, since it is not appropriate to bury the stool in this desert environment. Also, add water shoes to your packing list: you may decide to spend some time wading with your dog at one of the beachheads. When your dog is watered and leashed—and you have packed in drinking water for your hike—you are ready to cross the bridge and start on Verde River Trail 11.

The Old Verde River Sheep Bridge was once known as the Red Point Sheep Bridge. The structure is on the National Register of Historic Places, and was in fact used to move sheep between camps whenever they needed access to more forage. This bridge is a reconstruction of the original, which was damaged in a storm, built using the original towers.

Once you and your dog have crossed to the east side of the river, walk down the hill. There is no trailhead signage once you descend from the bridge. At the bottom of the hill, take a left (east), go over a small rise, and jog south. The very faint path here makes a wide turn, at which point you will be heading in a northward direction, which is your general trend for the remainder of the hike (excepting the odd switchback).

You are walking through a mesquite *bosque*, or forest. These desert riparian trees are capable of reaching fairly lofty heights because their roots grow meters deep and they can tap scarce water well beneath the desert floor. Also at the riverbanks are horsetails, sedges, and reeds.

At the lip of the *bosque*, 0.2 mile into the hike, you cross a wash to ascend a small hill. You come upon a trail junction at 0.4 mile: here the Willow Springs and Mazatzal Divide Trails take off to the right (east), while the Verde River Trail 11 forks left. You will cross a tributary at 0.5 mile that is easy to boulder hop or wade across—the rocks are loose so watch your footing. The path exits the stream to the right (east) and heads uphill again, but in no time, you turn north. At 0.5 mile, there is another trail junc-

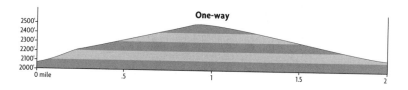

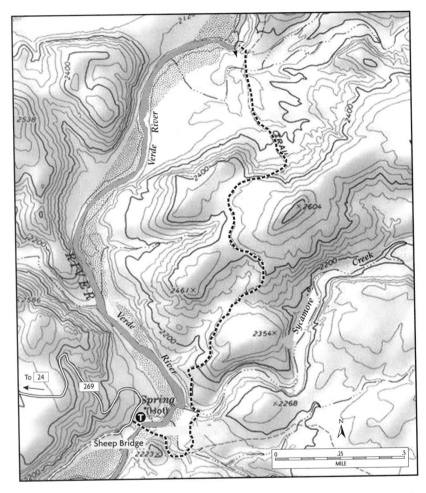

tion—the Dutchman Grave Trail is the rightward path and you stay north (forward) for the Verde River.

As you roll along this ridgeline away from the river, you encounter typical Sonoran Desert flora, such as the fragrant creosote, ocotillos, sages, cat-claw acacias, palo verde trees, saguaros, prickly pear cacti, and cholla cacti. Survey the cholla cacti closely—they are popular nest sites for cactus wrens. You can recognize a cactus wren's nest by its egg shape (larger than a goose, smaller than an ostrich) and small hole.

For such a remote place, the trail is amazingly clear of cacti, typically, but there are two brief patches of trail along the hilltop where foxtails

A very safe haven for a cactus wren's nestlings!

and brome grasses have established and apparently thrive. Curious noses are rewarded with sneezing fits and potentially dangerous infections from seed pods that lodge under the skin, so make sure your dog does not nose around in these grasses.

The trailbed itself alternates between rocky and compacted gravel surfaces. Some of the inclines are loose and rocky, but overall, for a desert trail, this is easy walking for both two- and four-legged hikers. The desert pavement beyond the trail is blanketed with a melange of bleached white, beige, pink, and russet gravel.

You cross another wash at 0.8 mile, and climb a rocky escarpment, after which the trail ascends a bit more. From here, you have a beautiful view of the west side of the canyon. The cliffs—like fused, dripping candles—are a mass of red and brown. As the river bends eastward, toward the trail, you cross another wash at 1.1 miles. Shortly, you begin to head downhill and at 1.3 miles, you cross a ravine—follow the cairns and head uphill once again. You top out here and you and your dog can enjoy some welcome shade cast by palo verde and mesquite trees. The trail all but vanishes briefly; but just veer left and downhill and you will pick up the path, which curves around the ridgeline. Shortly, the river appears below you, as well as the beach that will offer your dog a terrific play break at 2 miles before you both turn around and head back the way you came.

When you get back to Sheep Bridge, pass it, to go downhill (southward) on the wide path toward the river and explore this lush area of wide beaches and dispersed campsites. On warm days, your dog will appreciate this last splash break, as will you, before heading out.

PHOENIX AREA URBAN PARKS

42. Lookout Mountain Summit

Round trip: 1.2 miles
Hiking time: 1 hour
Difficulty: moderate
High point: 2054 feet
Elevation gain: 493 feet
Best: October through April
Map: Sunnyslope USGS
Contact: Phoenix Mountains Park and Recreation Area, (602) 262-7901

Getting there: To locate the trailhead, in Phoenix proceed to the intersection of Greenway Parkway and 16th Street; head south on 16th Street and follow the road up the mountain until it dead-ends at the trailhead.

In the 1960s, Phoenix conservationists rallied to create mountain parks and preserve the area's outdoor opportunities and scenic views. No one envisioned that the Phoenix Mountains Preserve would become one of the most heavily visited urban parks in the United States. Be assured that

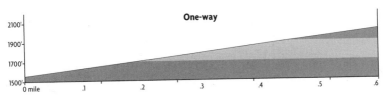

there are a few trails in these parks that you and your dog can enjoy without feeling as though you are in a Southwestern theme park. Lookout Mountain Summit Trail 150 takes you on a short climb up a mountain with scenic interest, varied Sonoran Desert plants and wildlife, and wide (albeit urban) vistas.

As with other desert hikes, take water along on this one. Even on cool winter days, full exposure can dehydrate both you and especially your dog in record time. In spring and fall, try to get on the trail early in the morning. You will stay cooler and see more wildlife.

Begin this hiker-only route on the wide path leading from the trailhead parking lot. The path narrows and begins a gentle ascent westward. A trail-conditioned dog will have no problem with the rocky path, which is steep and loose in places as you approach the flat-topped summit.

Like most of the mountain ranges in and around Phoenix, Lookout Mountain is largely made up of relatively young volcanic rock; even though the summit looks a bit like a volcanic cone from the trail, it is not. It is rather the result of a 1.5 million-year-old lava flow.

At 0.1 mile, you reach a trail junction with the perimeter trail, which allows horseback riding and mountain biking. Large outcroppings of volcanic boulders mark this junction and you can negotiate your dog into the shade cast should she need a water break at this early point. Follow the signpost markings (Trail 150), which lead you on a steadily rising

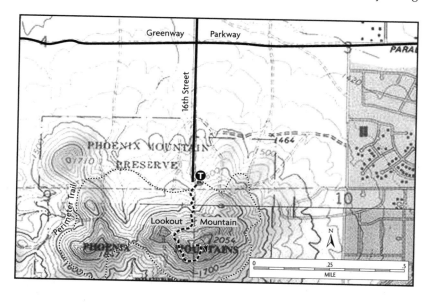

Even on a short winter hike, dogs get thirsty in this desert clime.

southwesterly path. Shortly, an (unmarked) trail veers off to the left—area users have blazed a steep shortcut to the top that you should avoid to continue westward on the summit path proper.

At just about 0.4 mile, you are far into the roughly three-quarter spiral to the summit and turning southeast. The climbing steepens, and you may not be able to convince your dog that your efforts are less strenuous than that of the climbers who can occasionally be spotted performing their graceful, roped ascents at the summit.

You top out at a quick 0.6 mile, but you should take some time for your dog to catch her breath and drink more water. While you do the same, enjoy the view before you. Phoenix is a city of suburbs, and few skyscrapers block your view of the city sights or the other parks in the preserve: Camelback Mountain sleeps to the southeast, almost obscuring Papago Park further behind it; Dreamy Draw, Piestewa Peak, and South Mountain Park are due south of you; and North Mountain Park is just to the southwest. Head back the way you came.

43. North Mountain National

Round trip: 3.2 miles
Hiking time: 2 hours
Difficulty: easy–moderate
High point: 1999 feet
Elevation gain: 509 feet
Best: October through April
Map: Sunnyslope USGS
Contact: Phoenix Mountains Park and Recreation Area, (602) 262-7901

Getting there: To get there, take 7th Street to Peoria Avenue and turn west into the park. Peoria becomes an interior park road; follow the winding road to the Maricopa Ramada on your right. The trailhead for North Mountain National Trail 44 is at the north end of the parking lot.

The rugged peaks and rolling desert of Phoenix's North Mountain Park once served as a popular campground for Indian School students and their families. The north central Phoenix area has changed, but the park remains a beautiful destination. While this hiking-only trail is within one of the least traveled parks in the Phoenix Mountains Preserve system (see Hike 42, Lookout Mountain Summit, for history of these parks), you should follow the leash rules both out of courtesy for other hikers and for your dog's protection, since some segments of the hike pass through areas with abundant, albeit urban-adapted, wildlife.

Bring adequate water and plan time for breaks, for this hike is exposed and contains some moderately steep grades. In fact, if you don't have a sun hat, you may not wish to leave the car. By turns, a rocky path and stone steps draw you into the summit trail before giving way to pavement (this road is still used to maintain communication towers) at the

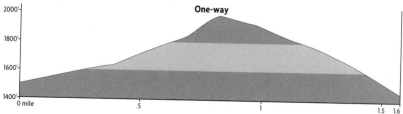

Cheryl and Didi at North Mountain

0.2-mile mark. The grade levels out only at the top of the summit, in about 0.6 mile.

While your way through these North Mountain peaks may not be wild, off-trail there are splendid examples of prime Sonoran Desert habitat which remain remarkably vital. Alongside the path, in the cooler mornings when wildlife are more active, your dog's eyes might follow a chuckwalla, jackrabbit, grey fox, ground squirrel, or Gambel's quail darting for cover. North Mountain Park boasts such thriving Sonoran Desert flora as brittlebush, creosote (enjoy their distinctive smell after monsoon rains), palo verde trees, bursage, jumping cholla cacti, saguaro cacti, and the thorny, flame-tipped ocotillos.

As you and your dog finish skirting the summit (1.1 miles), the road under paw and foot gives way to a rocky path with steep descents along a southeastern cut in North Mountain. The last 0.5 mile has some tricky footing, so be sure you have rested and watered before taking it on and heading back the way you came.

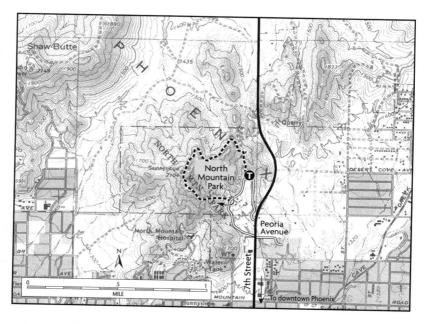

44. Mohave

Round trip: 3 miles
Hiking time: 2.5 hours
Difficulty: easy–moderate
High point: 1594 feet
Elevation gain: 200 feet
Best: October through April
Map: Sunnyslope USGS
Contact: Phoenix Mountains Park and Recreation Area (602) 262-7901
Note: Squaw Peak has recently been renamed in honor of fallen Hopi soldier Lori Piestewa; at publication, signage did not yet reflect this name change.

Getting there: To enjoy this scenic mountain park hike, take Glendale/Lincoln to 32nd Street and turn north. There is a small, signed, Phoenix Mountains Preserve parking lot immediately to your right. (If the lot is full, do not park in the residential area. Turn the hike around and begin from the Mohave terminus instead, which you reach by taking

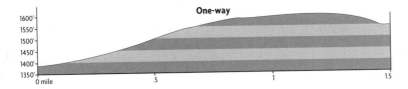

One-way

Glendale/Lincoln to just west of 24th Street and turning north on Squaw Peak Road. Continue 0.5 mile to the Mohave picnic ramada and Mohave Trail 200A.)

Thin clouds float too high to shade this craggy ridge along the Mohave Trail.

Water and leash your dog, pick up a spare Mutt Mitt from the handy dispenser, and you are ready to trek. From the south end of the trail, you will follow a path that scales a craggy saddle, then drops to the Mohave ramada. The trail first heads east, paralleling Lincoln Drive, then turns north to face the mountains. The gravel track under foot and paw is fairly even at the outset, but this multi-use path gets loose and rocky in places, so be sure to wear proper footgear and have your dog's booties handy.

At about 0.25 mile, the trail forks—take the westward route to continue on the Mohave Trail. You are switchbacking up the mountain's face surrounded by a lush swath of Sonoran Desert, with its complement of barrel cacti, bursage, palo verde trees, saguaros, ocotillos, buckhorn cholla, teddy bear cholla, and mammalaria cacti. Cactus wrens, quails, and mockingbirds contribute the sound effects.

The mountain range swells to fill the striking views to the north and

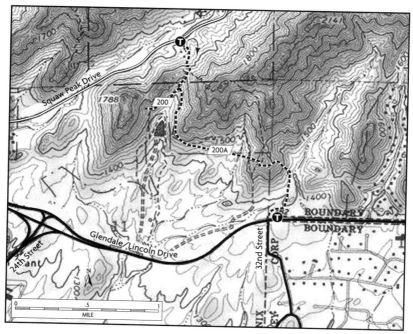

northwest. As you gain elevation, you take in ever more sweeping views of both the rugged mountain park and surrounding city—a study in contrasts. Occasionally, you will see blazed trails branching off. Trail users receive tickets for blazing or using blazed trails, so keep the leash and boots pointed along the Mohave Trail and enjoy the trip through the saddle.

Do not be surprised if your dog becomes more interested than usual in the boulders lining the trail. The jagged, fractured rocks here are prime chuckwalla habitat. When threatened, this cunning lizard wedges itself in rock fissures and "inflates" itself—it poses no threat to dogs. Research on the chuckwalla is conducted throughout the Phoenix Mountains Park and Recreation Area, and on spring mornings, you might be lucky enough to catch a chuckwalla sunning itself on boulder tops.

At 0.9 mile, you top out in elevation and are rewarded with terrific views of Piestewa Peak and the surrounding city. Your descent toward the Mohave terminus is moderately steep and the trail rocky. You will see at 1.2 miles a signed fork for Trail 200/200A—Trail 200 goes to the summit of a smaller peak to the southeast, and, water supply and energy permitting, you can easily add that 0.5 mile to your hike or continue to the terminus.

In this last 0.4 mile, the palo verde trees are a bit denser, cooling the trail a mite and offering shady rest areas for your dog. Of course, you can also use the ramada for a nice long shade and water break before turning back to your climb over the saddle and return to the trailhead.

45. Ranger

Round trip: 3 miles
Hiking time: 2 hours
Difficulty: moderate
High point: 2281 feet
Elevation gain: 714 feet
Best: October through April
Map: Lone Butte USGS map
Contact: Phoenix Mountains Park and Recreation Area, (602) 262-7901
Note: Depending on wind direction, gunfire reports from the nearby Phoenix police training facility can be heard from the Ranger Trail.

Getting there: To get there, go south on Central Avenue, which turns west and becomes the South Mountain Park perimeter road. Take a left at mile marker 1 and then a right at the Ranger Trail/Five Tables sign. Park here.

The lovely and expansive South Mountain Park, part of the Phoenix Mountains Preserve (see Hike 42, Lookout Mountain Summit), offers moderately challenging ascents, sweeping mountain and city views, and a wide range of Sonoran Desert plants and wildlife. You and your dog can start exploring this area with the Ranger Trail, a 1.5-mile scenic hike to the South Mountain National Trail. Though less busy than Phoenix's Camelback Trail, this is a multi-use trail—leash rules apply and just make good sense. Pack out waste and pack in plenty of water.

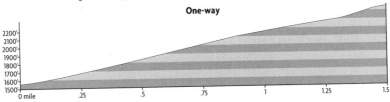

This exposed trail has a few steep ascents, giving two- and four-legged hikers a workout, but if you go in the morning, both you and your dog will appreciate the shade on this northwest face of the mountain.

From the parking lot the trailhead leads southwest toward the mountain on a very gentle gravel path. The trail becomes rockier in places—are your dog's booties handy?

In about 0.4 mile, after a small rise, you will cross the summit road. Here, long switchbacks wind you up the mountain. On your ascent, more of the city comes into view to the north and the long arm of South Mountain fills the view to the west. Closer in, notice the boulders that your dog is straining to sniff. Colorful lichens love the gneiss and schist rock types that dominate this area. The ferns tucked under boulders tend to die back during dry periods but spring to life after rains. In fact, the subtle beauty of this cactus and shrub-dotted landscape turns quite showy after rainy winters—the desert floor fairly bursts with wildflowers from March through April.

At trail's end, 1.5 miles up from the trailhead, do not be surprised if

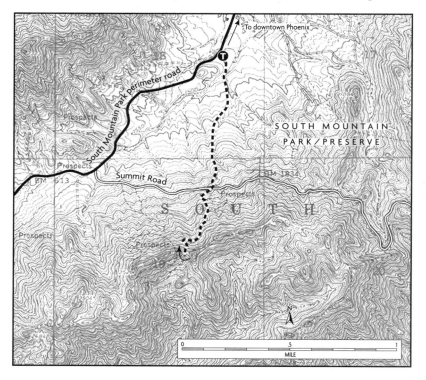

A sunrise jaunt along the Ranger Trail on South Mountain

you and your dog get buzzed by the camouflaged hover flies, which resemble bumble bees, the Sara orangetip butterfly, or red and black tarantula hawks. Naturalists have noticed that male tarantula hawks especially like these hilltop areas and are constantly on the lookout for mates—fortunately, they will not harass humans or dogs, so do not rush your trip back down the way you came on their account.

46. West Park Loop

Round trip: 4 miles
Hiking time: 2 hours
Difficulty: easy
High point: 1347 feet
Elevation gain: 77 feet
Best: October through April
Map: Tempe USGS Map
Contact: Papago Park Ranger, (602) 262-4599; Papago Park Manager, (602) 262-4837

Getting there: From Galvin Parkway North or South in Phoenix, take Papago Park Road west and park at the picnic ramada before you. If you have forgotten bags to pick up after your dog, Mutt Mitts are available. Once you have watered and leashed your dog—don't forget to pack water in—head west from the parking lot onto an unmarked dirt track; in 20 yards, you will pick up a northward gravel path, the West Park Loop Trail.

The unusual pink sandstone buttes in Papago Park have always caught the fancy of visitors and area residents, making the park's history as colorful as its trademark geologic oddities. A thousand years ago, the Hohokam used the park's most distinctive landmark, Hole-in-the-Rock, to mark solstices and equinoxes. In the nineteenth century, the federal government used the area as a temporary reservation for the Maricopa and Pima tribes. The area was designated a national monument in 1914 (Congress revoked monument status in 1932). During WWII, the park was still well outside Phoenix city limits, so the military erected a German prisoner-of-war camp on site; some of those buildings remain in use at the Phoenix Zoo.

Since Phoenix purchased the land in 1959, Papago Park's 1200 acres

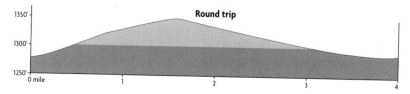

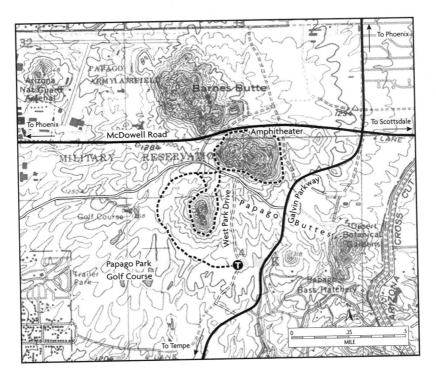

have offered a wondrously scenic setting for outdoor recreation. The lipstick-tinged buttes that rise up from the desert floor—known only as the "large" and "small" buttes—are the main features of this hike.

The trail follows a fence line between the park and Papago Golf Course for 0.3 mile; at the fork, head north to approach the buttes in a clockwise manner. Once on the loop, you wind through a prickly landscape of cat-claw acacias and Christmas cacti. The path is easy on boot and paw, however, keep an eye on your dog's curious nose! Palo verde and iron-wood trees cast thin shade on occasion, but plan to break out the water bowl on this hike, and take a lot with you—the trail is exposed except directly under the shadows of the buttes and there is no water available between the ramadas.

You will see the occasional blazed trail branching off more directly toward the buttes, but why hurry? (In fact, blazed trail travel is not allowed in the preserve.) Follow the signposts and keep your leash pointed down the longer path through this scenic desertscape. At 1.1 miles, find a marked fork—follow the rightward path, which first traverses the west

A view of the large butte from West Park Loop

side of the large butte. Shortly, you start trekking through dry washes that seasonal rains, coursing off of the buttes, cut into the desert.

Rock hounds in particular will delight in this section of the trail, which scales the haunches of the large butte and affords a close look at the sedimentary sandstone comprising these landforms. These relatively young (6- to 15-million-year-old) rocks are chock full of iron oxide (hematite), and what the eye sees is captivating: compressed red sandstone, flecks of granite, and rainwater erosion holes (called tafoni) that give the buttes their sea-of-holes facades.

While the urban setting means that you are more likely to see ground squirrels or jackrabbits scurrying amongst the bushes than hear the yips of coyotes, raptors such as hawks can often be spied soaring or perching on the buttes, and the occasional falcon pays a visit as well. So keep your eyes peeled for wildlife.

At just over 2 miles along a short stretch paralleling McDowell Road is an historic stone amphitheater built by the Civilian Conservation Corps. Once used for sunrise Easter services, it now serves as an excellent rest and play stop along the trail.

Head south toward Elliot Ramada and the small butte once you round the curve of the large butte. At just under 3 miles, after you and your dog have had your fill of shade and water, head out of the ramada continuing south—you will see a series of signs marking an orienteering course. Turn east to follow the start of the loop back to the trailhead.

47. Lousley Hill

Round trip: 1.2 miles
Hiking time: 1 hour
Difficulty: easy
High point: 2032
Elevation gain: 232
Best: October through April
Map: McDowell Peak USGS
Contact: McDowell Mountain Regional Park, (480) 471-0173

Getting there: Getting there from Phoenix is a snap. Take Shea Boulevard east about 15 miles to Fountain Hills Boulevard and head north (left)—this road becomes McDowell Mountain Road. Turn west (left)

onto McDowell Mountain Park Drive, proceed to the fee station (day use fee of $5.00 per vehicle is required), and follow the road as it turns north. Turn right (east) onto Lousley Drive South, and turn right into the Lousley Hill trailhead parking area. Remember to bring along a bag so that you can pack out waste. After you've watered and leashed your pooch, you're ready to go.

Once an important hunting-gathering site for the Hohokam people, the McDowell Mountain Regional Park is now a popular destination for those seeking stunning views and outdoor adventure.

Lousley Hill would be fun even if you were just looking to keep your dog's pads conditioned for more strenuous trails that are inaccessible during peak winter snow season. The panoramic views here—the McDowells to the west, Four Peaks to the east—are their own draw, however.

One of the things that you early bird, hiker-dog teams will like about this 1.2 mile loop is the amount of shade the return trip offers just as the desert begins to warm up. Another plus for your dog is that this is a hiking-only trail, so that there are fewer opportunities for conflict with horses and mountain bikes in this popular desert park. Leash rules apply and for your dog's protection, follow them—typically, cacti reward curiosity with injury.

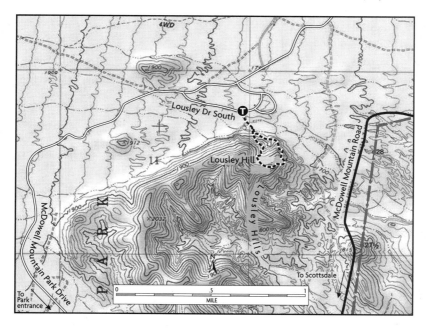

The McDowell Mountains from Lousley Hill

From the trailhead, you and your dog will take the wide gravel path that follows a southward arc through an arroyo, or floodplain, among palo verde trees and saguaro cacti.

At the marked loop fork, take the left trail to ascend Lousley Hill from its northern arm. This rocky footpath is moderately steep, sure to elicit a few huffs and pants. Even in winter, bring plenty of water since much of this trail along your ascent is exposed.

You finish your climb at 0.6 mile and follow the trail as it circles the summit of Lousley Hill. This stretch of trail along the hilltop will remind you why the old tourism slogan for Phoenix—"the Valley of the Sun"—became fixed: as far as you can see, mountains rise above the sun-drenched desert (and desert cities) like waves on an ancient seabed.

Your way back is a series of gentle switchbacks along the western face of Lousley Hill. Enjoy the silent company of the McDowell Mountains, immediately to your left, as you and your dog take this last 0.5-mile segment back to the trailhead.

48. Wagner Loop

Round trip: 4.7 miles
Hiking time: 3 hours
Difficulty: easy
High point: 2214 feet
Elevation gain: 240 feet
Best: October through April
Map: McDowell Peak USGS
Contact: McDowell Mountain Regional Park, (480) 471-0173

Getting there: To get to the Wagner trailhead from Phoenix, take Shea Boulevard east approximately 15 miles to Fountain Hills Boulevard and head north (left)—this road becomes McDowell Mountain Road. Turn west (left) onto McDowell Mountain Park Drive, proceed to the fee station (day use fee of $5.00 per vehicle is required), and follow the road as it turns north. Turn left at Pallisades Drive, approximately 2 miles into the park; if the "campground full" sign is on the road at Pallisades, ignore it—there is a separate parking area for the trailhead, which is on your right, almost immediately, at the kiosk.

Once your dog is watered and leashed, prepare for a delightful roll among the flats and foothills of the McDowell Mountains that is easy on paw and boot. Desert hiking cautions still apply (some wildlife and

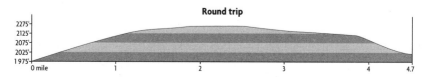

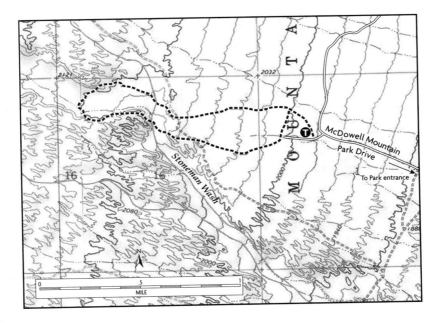

plants can reward your dog's curiosity with injury), as do courtesies, so heed the leash rule on the entire hike, and bring a bag so that you can pick up after your dog.

You head out from Wagner Loop trailhead on an initially northward path that is fairly wide and made up of broken down granite gravel. You will see the campground on your left during this part of the hike and pass two campground spur trails on your way to the Granite Trail, the second piece of the four-legged loop that you and your dog are enjoying.

From the desert environs and wildlife here—palo verde trees, jojoba, saguaros, creosote, jackrabbits, Gambel's quail, and coyotes—you might already expect that the hike is almost completely exposed except for wash areas and boulder outcroppings. Make sure for your dog's health and safety to heed the seasonal hiking recommendations, and of course, pack in plenty of water and allow extra time for shade breaks.

The Wagner Loop Trail takes you across a minor wash at 0.7 mile, then crosses Pallisades Drive at the 1 mile mark—both crossings are signed. The views are spectacular: looming over the trail ahead is Rock Knob and the entire McDowell mountain range.

The trail has been taking you west, but once you come upon the signed Granite Trail junction at the 1.1-mile mark, you turn north. On this more

A winter extravagance: Chuparosa along the Granite Trail

remote segment, you see more examples of the Sonoran Desert's rich plant diversity: barrel cacti, ocotillo, chain fruit cholla, teddy bear cholla, and hedgehog cacti. Along the middle section of the Granite Trail (1.7 miles) and as you turn counterclockwise (west, then south), you encounter lush and scenic rocky outcrops brimming with the red blooms of the chuparosa—a pretty, succulent plant popular with butterflies. This is a convenient break spot if you and your dog are ready.

Your trail turns east at the 2.2-mile mark as you take a left onto the Bluff Trail. A gentle descent takes you back down to the desert floor atop a toe of the foothills. The eastern horizon offers a clear view of beautiful local landmarks and remote wilderness—from here, you can easily make out Red Mountain, Four Peaks, and the Mazatzal Mountains. At approximately 3 miles, a cairn marks an otherwise unsigned path; keep heading east here to cross Stoneman Wash and join up with the Granite Trail again, which you intersect at 3.3 miles. Take a right onto the Granite Trail, then follow the sign to the campground and take the south loop. This route conveniently leads directly to a comfort station; turn left to arrive back at the Wagner trailhead.

If you want to extend your hike, or if you prefer to avoid the campground, take a left onto the Granite Trail from the Bluff Trail and then you will take a right at the Wagner junction to reach the trailhead—this would be the only repeated segment on your hike.

The Granite and Bluff Trail segments on this loop are open to cyclists and horses as well as hikers, but since the entire loop is relatively flat, conflicts with cyclists are less frequent than you might expect in a busy urban park. By heeding the leash requirement, you and Fido will have a terrific time sharing with others this gem of a loop trail.

49. Wind Cave

Round trip: 3.2 miles
Hiking time: 2 hours
Difficulty: easy–moderate
High point: 2800 feet
Elevation gain: 800 feet
Best: October through April
Map: Apache Junction USGS
Contact: Usery Mountain Regional Park Supervisor, (480) 984-0032
Note: Depending on wind direction, gunfire reports from the Usery Mountain Shooting Range can be heard from the Wind Cave Trail.

Getting there: In Phoenix take the Superstition Freeway (US Hwy 60) about 21 miles to Ellsworth Road and head north; Ellsworth becomes Usery Pass Road. Continue on Usery Pass Road 1.5 miles past McDowell Road and turn right into Usery Park. Follow Usery Park Drive to the fee station ($5.00 per vehicle) and then proceed to Wind Cave Drive. Turn left and follow Wind Cave Drive to picnic area 8 and the parking area.

To enjoy the popular trail to Wind Cave, you do not have to be a geology buff. You only have to appreciate the fact that a splendid mix of time, wind, rain, and rock have formed a unique and scenic feature on Pass Mountain. Of course, feel free to learn the geology and give your dog a

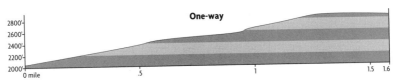

tutorial on this easy Sonoran Desert hike. Or the two of you can just take to the trail and bask in the mild desert clime.

Wind Cave Trail starts out as a level, manicured desert path that wanders through a green harmony of bursage, creosote, and cacti. Heed the leash requirement in Usery Park; while Wind Cave Trail is a hiking-only trail, it can be busy on weekends, and you are likely to encounter other trekkers (and dogs). Using a leash is a safety issue for your four-legged companion as well. Remember, even a maintained trail such as this one is not entirely tame—avoid a confrontation with desert plants to keep Fido's paws and nose spine-free.

From the 0.4-mile mark to just over 1 mile, you and your dog encounter a series of gently climbing switchbacks that gain nearly all of the elevation on this hike. At 1.2 miles, the trail turns southeast and follows a fairly level grade for the remainder of the hike up to the Wind Cave. Here, the cliff blocks the morning sun, but since most of the terrain on this hike is exposed—and certainly if you go in the afternoon—bring

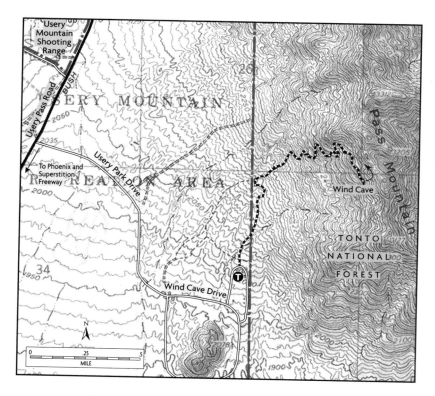

After a drink and a rest at Wind Cave, Gracie and Ebony head back down the trail.

plenty of water to prevent you and your dog from dehydrating.

The last 0.4 mile to the Wind Cave is a scenic ramble skirting a lichen-kissed cliff wall. If you visit in spring, it is not unusual to be serenaded by trilling rock wrens or buzzed by Costas hummingbirds along your way.

Wind Cave is actually a large depression formed by slowly eroding layers of granite and volcanic tuff in Pass Mountain, and as you make a final turn into the cave, your dog will be ready for more water and perhaps a treat and play time. Bold antelope ground squirrels often provide entertainment here, but resist the urge to reward them with food—and be sure to keep your dog under control at all times.

Take time before heading back the way you came to enjoy the welcome shade and wide vista from Wind Cave. Northward, the views encompass the rugged terrain of Tonto National Forest and the scenic McDowell Mountains. Directly below you and southward lies the entire Usery Park Recreation Area. You might think you have seen a mirage among the developments of Fountain Hills to the northwest, but what you have just witnessed is the hourly spouting of the 560-foot fountain—one of the world's tallest—at Fountain Lake.

50. Waterfall Canyon

Round trip: 1.8 to 3.3 miles
Hiking time: 1 to 2 hours
Difficulty: easy
High point: 1838
Elevation gain: 358 feet
Best: September through April
Map: White Tank Mountains USGS
Contact: White Tank Mountain Regional Park, (623) 935-2505

Getting there: In Phoenix, go west on Dunlap/Olive Avenue, which leads into White Tank Mountain Regional Park. Just past the gate and fee station

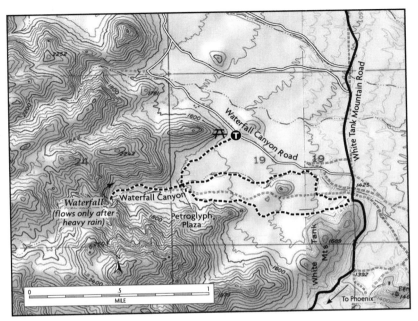

($5.00 per car), Olive becomes White Tank Mountain Road and turns north. Proceed to Waterfall Canyon Road, turn left, and park at the trailhead. As always in desert environs, take along a bag so you can pick up after Fido.

The hidden, ephemeral waterfall at the end of Waterfall Canyon Trail is both a treat and a tease to desert dwellers. Drawn in by the promise of water in an otherwise sizzling clime, hikers and dogs alike enjoy Waterfall Canyon's frequent shady spots thanks to gargantuan, lichen-clad boulders and desert trees. The trail's end is the real reward for your dog, though: sheer cliffs cast welcome shadows on three sides of this natural grotto.

Enough water for your dog to cool her pads is commonly found at the bottom of the 80-foot-high waterfall even weeks after the rains have left the Sonoran Desert behind. The hum and flutter of native bees and tarantula hawks add to the pleasant ambiance of this desert oasis. Once your dog is leashed and watered—pack in plenty for both of you since the waterfall flows heavily only after a hard rain—you are ready to set out on this short but scenic Sonoran Desert hike.

The Maricopa County leash requirement dovetails with common sense desert hiking: rattlesnakes, scorpions, jackrabbits, cactus wrens, Gila monsters, mourning doves, and roadrunners are abundant, even in these park

Razzberri Jones at White Tank Mountain Regional Park (photo by David R. Newton)

islands adrift in the sprawling Phoenix metropolis. You'll want to keep your dog close to protect her and alert you to any wildlife that her ears and eyes sense before you do.

The barrier-free, compacted granite trail gives way to natural desert pavement and river rocks at the 0.4-mile mark. Here, a shade pavilion known as Petroglyph Plaza draws attention to some of the remarkable rock art found throughout this park. Believed to be left behind by the Hohokam as long ago as 300 A.D., the petroglyphs invite a contemplative moment or two for you as your dog enjoys a welcome water break.

For the shorter up-and-back route, continue straight (west) into Waterfall Canyon and begin your gentle climb toward the mountain, winding under lacy-leaved palo verde and ironwood trees.

To extend your hike and enjoy a more remote trail segment, you will follow the left (southward) trail at the pavilion for 0.2 mile. Take the left fork for 0.4 mile, pick up a paved, barrier-free trail which turns right (south) for 0.2 mile, then head back on the right (west) path for 0.7 mile to the pavilion junction, for a total of 1.5 miles for loop. Here, you turn left to pick up the trail into Waterfall Canyon.

Most of the easy ascent to the 80-foot waterfall comes in the last 0.3 mile as you close in on the mountainside. If you are hiking within a day or two of a heavy rain, the waterfall should still be flowing into the pool at the trail's end. The memory of desert rain beckons both humans and canines to take a romp and a rest before turning back to face the sun. You return to the pavilion the way you came and then take the main trail on the left (northeastward) back to the trailhead.

BLACK MESA AND PERRY MESA

51. Agua Fria National Monument

Round trip: 3.5 miles
Hiking time: 2 hours
Difficulty: easy–moderate
High point: 3133 feet
Elevation change: 100 feet
Best: October through April
Maps: Cordes Junction and Joes Hill USGS
Contact: Bureau of Land Management, Phoenix Field Office,
(602) 580-5500
Note: Area subject to flash flooding; river crossings can be dangerous especially after rains—always check conditions before setting out.

Getting there: From Phoenix, drive about 45 miles north on Interstate 17 to head east (right) at exit 256 onto Badger Springs Wash Road. You will see an information kiosk for the Agua Fria National Monument upon turning; the trailhead is another mile from this point. Continue on the

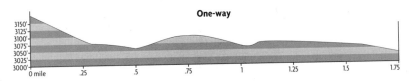

One-way

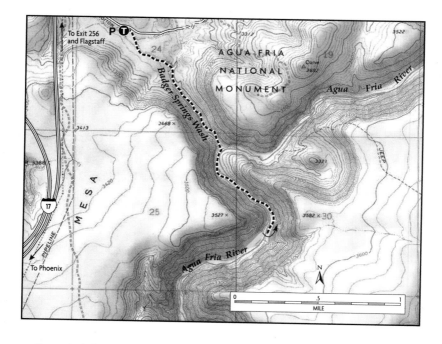

well-graded dirt road until you see a cleared area outlined by boulders before a T intersection. Park here.

A leash is not required as long as your dog responds to voice commands, but keep it handy in case you encounter other trail users or wildlife such as javelina or deer, which range here. Be aware that rattlesnakes and venomous lizards live nearby; be sure of your dog's ability to respond to voice command and keep her close to you, especially among the bouldery riverbanks that make up much of your trail beyond Badger Springs Wash.

Once your dog is watered and under control, you are ready for your beautiful river canyon ramble. Walk down the right fork of this inter-section (south) toward the canyon and in about 150 feet, you will see a sign and a registration box—please sign in. From this trailhead, you and your dog head nearly due south into Badger Springs Wash—follow the wash. The wide sandy path is partially shaded by bluffs rising up ini-tially only on your right, then on both sides as you proceed into the

Opposite: A scenic and rugged desert river lends the Agua Fria National Monument both its name and its main attraction.

canyon separating Black Mesa and Perry Mesa. Even in dry periods, the wash may be slushy, so be sure to wear water-compatible or waterproof footgear with good ankle support. In spite of the even elevation on this hike, this canyon is quite rugged. Large, flat boulders encroach upon the trail; they seem to have slid down from the hills like pieces of some vast, stony glacier. The cliffs above are made up of rocks as neatly "stacked" as pre-fab masonry, an odd and imposing symmetry in a wild place.

The wash meets up with the Agua Fria River at 0.8 mile in the middle of a wide, westward bend in the canyon. Looking upstream to your left and northeast, you see what appears to be a mirror image of the route you will take downstream to the right and southeast: basalt-covered cliffs dotted with cacti (at the northernmost part of their range, some impressive saguaros are found along this trail) and skirted by tamarisks, Arizona sycamores, and cottonwoods.

You and your dog will enjoy bounding across the river at this fairly shallow point—rest assured this is not the last crossing or splash break you will make! In fact, only once, at the 1-mile mark, are you separated from the riverbank by thick vegetation. Once boot and paw ascend the left bank of the Agua Fria River, turn right to go downstream and you will immediately pick up a faint footpath if your dog has not already sniffed it out.

From here, the hike is essentially yours to determine, depending on river levels and flow rates, and your dog's conditioning and size—some fairly major boulder-hopping will be necessary if the river is high, particularly at 1.1 and 1.4 miles. But the reward is a gem of a half-day hike where nearly every 50 feet offers a new vantage point to enjoy a wild, perennial southwestern river. The stark contrast between the dazzling whites and grays of river rocks and the coffee-colored basalt topping Perry Mesa is a visual feast. Ephemeral pools and plenty of convenient crossings (at the 1.3, 1.4, and 1.5-mile marks, especially) ensure an enjoyable outing for you and your four-legged companion in and along the river bottoms.

When you approach the 1.75-mile mark, the trail has taken you along a large bend in the river, just past some wide beaches with great access to the river, shady spots, and gigantic tabletop boulders suitable for a rest or picnic break. If you have not packed in your water, you must treat any that you draw from the river. Enjoy the scramble back the way you came.

PRESCOTT AREA

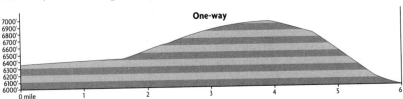

52. Oaks and Willows

Round trip: 12 miles
Hiking time: 7 hours
Difficulty: moderate–difficult
High point: 7008 feet
Elevation change: 1008 feet
Best: March through November
Maps: Juniper Mountain and Indian Peak USGS
Contact: Prescott National Forest, Chino Valley Ranger Station,
  (928) 636-2302

Getting there: In Prescott, take Williamson Valley Road north; beyond city limits, this road is known as Forest Road 6. When you pass mile point 43, FR 7 is to your left (west)—take FR 7 to its end, 0.6 mile beyond Pine Spring, and park here at the trailhead for Oaks and Willows Trail 3. High clearance is recommended for FR 7.

Most of your hike traverses the typically dry folds and plateaus of the Juniper Mesa Wilderness. This is a hiking and horseback-riding trail only, and it receives fairly light use. Make sure your dog is well watered after the car ride, leash her up, and pack in extra water. You head southwest from the parking area and enter the wilderness area right away, following the old jeep road that makes up your path along the Pine Creek drainage.

Under this close forest of oaks and junipers (both the one-seed and alligator varieties), it is shady and cool. This segment of the hike is an easy climb to Juniper Mesa, initially along a gravelly footpath. Typical of desert backcountry trails—particularly ones that feature any elevation change—the trailbed is a combination of surfaces with compacted forest floor giving way to rocky stretches reminiscent of untrodden desert pavement.

You will cross several washbeds before you reach the 1.5-mile mark, but the trail is easy to pick out each time and keeps to a steady, southwesterly, uphill course. Ferns peek around boulders here, so be sure that your dog avoids nibbling fronds that could make her sick.

Autumn is the prettiest time to visit this trail, with its cooler temperatures and changing leaves. Spring is a close runner-up, however, thanks to mild temperatures, showy wildflowers, and the neon light cast by the tender new leaves of the Gambel oaks. Once you ascend Juniper Mesa, you will understand why it is important to check summertime temperatures before planning your trip: this trail gets hot. The plateau offers pretty views and level but exposed trekking.

At roughly halfway (3 miles), you come upon a junction with the Juniper Mesa Trail 20, which runs east–west through the wilderness. You will make a rightward (northwesterly) turn to continue along the Oaks and Willows Trail 3 and traverse the mesa. In 1.5 miles, you make a moderately

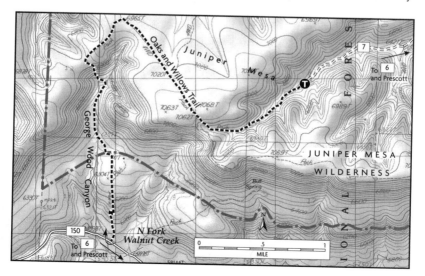

steep drop as you head south into George Wood Canyon, a thickly wooded and shady nook of the Juniper Mountains. Places for you and your dog to enjoy a break abound on this level section from 5 to 5.5 miles.

Your last descent is much more exposed and, again, moderately steep. Rocky stretches are common here; slow and easy does it, and be sure to take plenty of water breaks, for the broad, sparsely vegetated meadows are dotted with squat junipers that cast little shade near the trail. The path ends at the trailhead accessed by FR 150 (6 miles) and just above the north fork of Walnut Creek. When you are ready, point the leash uphill and hike out the way you came.

A pretty—and shady—pine-oak woodland keeps tails wagging along your way up to Juniper Mesa.

It is common for these creeks and springs to be dry, but if you are hiking after winter or monsoon rains, you and your dog will be able to enjoy splash breaks at either end of the hike; purify what you take to drink from these untreated water sources.

53. Woodchute

Round trip: 6.5 miles
Hiking time: 3.5 hours
Difficulty: easy–moderate
High point: 7707 feet
Elevation change: 682 feet
Best: March through November
Maps: Munds Draw and Hickey Mountain USGS
Contact: Prescott National Forest, Chino Valley Ranger Station, (928) 636-2302

Getting there: To get there from Prescott, follow State Hwy 89A north approximately 25 miles and take a left at the Potato Patch Campground/

Picnic Summit turnoff (0.5 mile past the Mingus Recreation Area turn-off). The road forks; take the left fork uphill to Forest Road 106. Park in the lot near the gate which blocks vehicular access to FR 106. After your dog has taken a drink and you have packed in water for the trail, head north on FR 106 0.5 mile to the trailhead. FR 106 forks to the right into a turnabout—this is your trailhead for Woodchute Trail 102.

The views from atop Woodchute Mountain are highly scenic, and so is your way there. The footpath winds northward through chapparal and mixed conifer forests characterized by scrub oak, manzanita, alligator juniper, prickly pear cacti, Gambel oaks, and ponderosa pines. Porous volcanic rocks sporting colorful colonies of lichens make faces at you from the trailsides. Wet winters yield dazzling and abundant spring wildflowers; oaks lend autumn color to this high desert landscape.

You start out in a fairly heavy pine forest and pass through a gate affixed to two ponderosas to enter the Woodchute Wilderness. The trail is a comfortable, compacted path dusted here and there with cinder or gravel; a few loose, rocky segments pop up on the steeper inclines/declines, so watch your footing. At 0.8 mile from the parking area, the first of many beautiful views opens up—on a clear day here, you can see the red rock cliffs surrounding Sedona. Just off trail, ascend a promontory guarded by ponderosa pines and a giant alligator juniper with cacti growing at its feet; visible from here are the road in the tree-lined canyon below you and the San Francisco Peaks to the north.

Back on trail, you and your dog begin to traverse a wide ridgeback, and views of Chino Valley and Juniper Mesa open up to your left. The trail zigzags to the left and right side of this ridge and shade is intermittent here, but frequently a venerable alligator juniper proffers a good spot for a water break. Keep alert for rattlesnakes.

The folds of Woodchute Mountain roll nearer, and the cliffs and rocks flush pink as you climb. You lose a tiny bit of elevation just past 1.5 miles and there are strong, cooling winds here. As you and your dog begin another gentle climb, the cliffs rise to your left. Beautiful, jutting,

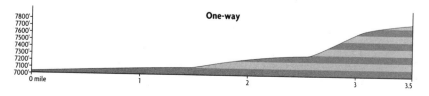

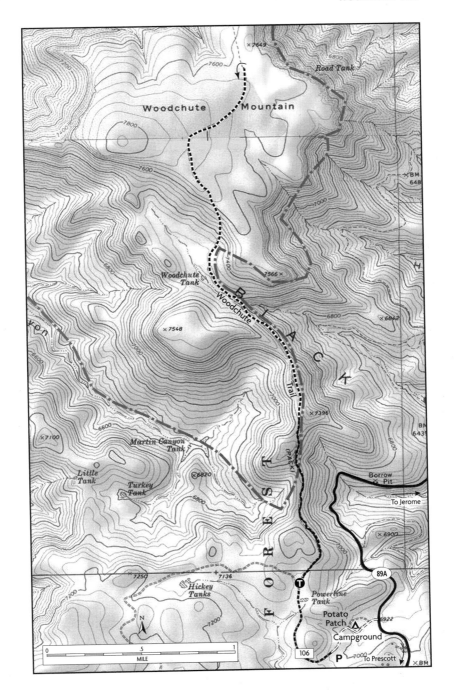

espresso-brown rocks poke out from the opposite walls of the canyon.

At just past 2.5 miles, your climb to the top begins in earnest. The reward comes at 3 miles when you and your dog are once again tucked under the intermittent shade of an open ponderosa forest. Enjoy the wide views here as you explore the crest of Woodchute Mountain. The trail continues for another 3.5 miles, but it is a steep and rocky descent. Assess your dog's conditioning—and your water supply—before exploring this part of the trail; when you are ready, head back south the way you came.

Native bees hum a springy tune among the high-desert blooms in the Woodchute Wilderness.

SIERRA ANCHA FOREST

54. Parker Creek

Round trip: 5 miles
Hiking time: 3.5 hours
Difficulty: moderate–difficult
High point: 7000 feet
Elevation gain: 1890
Best: March through November
Map: Aztec Peak USGS
Contact: Tonto National Forest, Pleasant Valley Ranger Station,
(928) 462-4300

Getting there: To get to the trailhead, proceed from Claypool (between Miami and Globe) on State Hwy 188 for approximately 15 miles to Hwy 288. Go north (right) on Hwy 288 for approximately 19.7 miles to the Sierra Ancha Experiment Station. Much of this road is unpaved, but it is well enough maintained that high-clearance vehicles are not necessary. You will see a Forest Service sign (Trail 160) just beyond the Arizona Department of Transportation facility turnoff, where you turn right into a small parking lot.

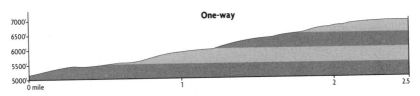

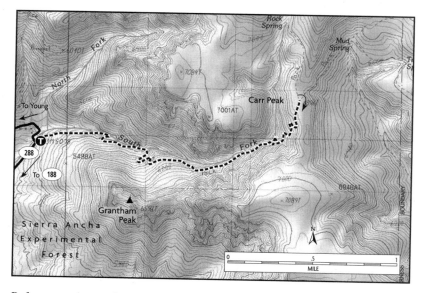

Before you leave, be sure your dog is well watered and that you pack plenty of water in; the trail climbs away from the creek past the 0.7-mile mark. Parker Creek flows through the Sierra Ancha Experimental Forest—a name which connotes a very large laboratory with trees under glass. Actually, the research area was established to study different ways to manage forest watersheds. The site was selected because it was representative of several different desert ecosystems, including the chaparral semi-desert and ponderosa pine forest you and your dog will travel through on this hike. The forest shade keeps your dog happy on the trail, and she can have a splash on the way out to cool her pads. The views, particularly on the accessible overlook points at the lower and upper ends of the hike, are spectacular and stretch all the way south to Four Peaks. Closer in, you can see local landmarks like Lake Roosevelt to the south, Armer Mountain, and Carr Peak.

Your ascent begins right away. The forest is a haven for wildlife: even this close to the trailhead, you might see white-tailed deer (or deer sign). Though bears and wild turkeys are elusive, they do roam here; so heed the leash rule and stay alert.

The trail is fairly even and well maintained, but leaf litter and pine duff obscure rocks on the trail, so watch your footing. Wide switchbacks

Opposite: Lichen-drenched columns tower over a tricky boulderfall on the Parker Creek trail.

on this section warm you up for the significant elevation change on this hike. The one tricky spot on the hike is a set of boulderfalls 0.1 mile apart, beginning at the 1.8-mile mark. The trail is straight across, but not all of the rocks are stable, so test where you are putting your feet and keep your dog close at heel. This would be a treacherous area during or after even a gentle rain—be sure to check weather conditions before setting out on this hike.

At about mile 2, your workout intensifies and the switchbacks tighten. As you and Fido climb, enjoy crossing (and dropping into) two drainages. Impressive boulders jut from the mountainside onto the trail ledge here. Agaves cling to these outcrops, even as you ascend into ponderosa pine forest. This juxtaposition reminds you that you are in a transition zone from one desert landform to another.

The last mile of the official Parker Creek Trail traverses areas damaged by the 2000 Coon fire which have recently undergone some rehabilitation; you may continue for that last mile or end the hike at 2.5 miles, where your huffing and panting are rewarded with wide views. The way you came is the way out.

WESTERN DESERTS

55. Harquahala Mountain Summit

Round trip: 12 miles
Hiking time: 7 hours
Difficulty: difficult
High point: 5681 feet
Elevation gain: 3290 feet
Best: October through April
Map: Socorro Peak and Harquahala Mountain USGS
Contact: Bureau of Land Management, Phoenix Field Office,
    (623) 580-5500

Getting there: From Phoenix, take US Hwy 60 northwest about 50 miles through Wickenburg and then due west to Aguila. As you exit Aguila, check your odometer and proceed 13.6 miles (if you pass mile marker 72, you have gone too far). Take a left, go through the gate, which must be closed behind you, and proceed 2 miles on this rough, four-wheel-drive road to a barricade with a tiny parking area. This is your trailhead, though it is unsigned.

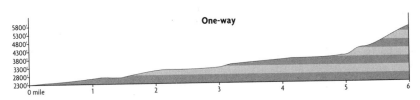

The Harquahala Mountain summit path might seem easy since you and your dog begin by padding along an old mule trail, but with 3290 feet of elevation gain and a rocky trail surface, it is a true challenge. Plan to start early, pack in lots of water, and be confident of your dog's conditioning before setting out. As always, when visiting fragile desert environments, pick up after your dog. Leashes are not required here as long as your dog responds unfailingly to voice commands, but keep the leash handy as a courtesy to other trail users you may encounter. The summit is accessible by another route, and it is there that you will likely meet other visitors.

From the trailhead, follow the path uphill (southeast). Keeping you and your dog company are many familiar Sonoran Desert denizens—towering saguaros, cholla and hedgehog cacti, ocotillos, creosote bushes, and palo verde and mesquite trees. Do not be surprised if you happen upon a Gila monster sunning itself on a rocky perch, or if you get buzzed by native bees on your water breaks. You are skirting the Harquahala Mountains Wilderness Area boundary here, but your eyes will be fooled: certainly all of this scenic, thriving landscape fits the definition of "wild."

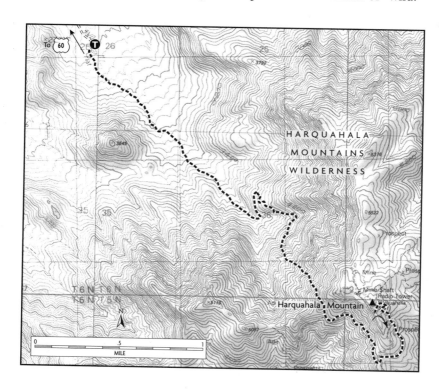

The Harquahala Mountains offer a challenging summit through a desert wonderland.

Your steady climb comes to an end at approximately the same time you cross into the wilderness area with a sharp northward turn. Head southeast again and from here, your climb is a fast burn to the summit. At this point you are probably wondering whether you and Fido would have more enjoyed a drive to the summit from one of the old mining roads in the area. Take heart and take your time, with plenty of rest and water breaks, to enjoy the spectacular views of this rugged terrain. As you catch your breath and your dog drinks her fill, take out your field glasses. Desert bighorn sheep live here, and they particularly love craggy summits; but these shy, agile creatures have excellent eyesight and will typically scamper uphill at the first sign of encroachment—chances are, you will not get a good look at them without your binoculars.

The trail turns east at approximately 4.2 miles, then heads southeast once more at 5.5 miles as you approach your last climb. You slip outside the Harquahala Wilderness Area again just before reaching the summit. Though today microwave towers grace Harquahala's crown, it is hard to believe that a solar observatory was once located on this remote mountaintop: only ruins remain from the Smithsonian Astrophysics Observatory, and the site is on the National Register of Historic Places. Enjoy a break here—and stunning views of Sunset Pass and Browns Canyon to the northeast—before turning back the way you came.

56. Ben Avery to Indian Spring

Round trip: 7 miles
Hiking time: 3.5 hours
Difficulty: easy
High point: 1834 feet
Elevation gain: 251 feet
Best: October through April
Map: Eagletail Mountains West USGS
Contact: Bureau of Land Management, Yuma Field Office,
   (928) 317-3200

Getting there: Drive west from Phoenix approximately 80 miles on Interstate 10 to exit 81, then turn left to go over the freeway and follow Harquahala Valley Road right (due south) toward Harquahala Valley. In 5 miles, turn right (west) onto Courthouse Rock Road (also called Centennial); check your odometer here. At a fork at about 6.8 miles, veer right onto a gas pipeline road to head northwest. In another 3.8 miles (10.8 miles from the Courthouse Rock turnoff), turn left onto the four-wheel-drive, signed road heading into the Eagletail Mountains Wilderness. Drive 1.5 miles and park at the kiosk—this is the north terminus trailhead for the Ben Avery Trail.

The Ben Avery Trail, named for a noted Arizona outdoor enthusiast and writer, leads through dramatically hued volcanic basalt hills rising up from the *bajadas* of the rugged Eagletail Mountains. There are grace notes here, however. Natural arches and rock spires can be viewed from the trail, and the sweet scents of the fall- and spring-blooming, bitter condalia trees waft over the desert.

Once you have grabbed a bag and your dog is watered and under good voice control (keep the leash handy), you are ready to set out. Be sure you have brought plenty of water since much of your route is exposed and Indian Spring at trail's end is not likely to be flowing except during the wettest seasons. Proceed south from the kiosk through the fence and follow the path west. The trail is a combination of old jeep roads, washes, and desert footpaths that are fairly comfortable under boot and conditioned paws. Stately Courthouse Rock, a popular rock climbing spot, will be on your left.

The trail soon begins to follow a scenic wash to your left—huge creosote bushes crowd the boulder piles lining the walls of this minicanyon. Your path quickly turns west. Before you have gone 1 mile, the trail dips into the wash and you will continue along the washbed, generally westward, for about 0.75 mile. It is fairly easy to find shade thanks to the high walls and the old-growth palo verde and mesquite trees that line the wash cuts. You see several pretty, shrubby stone grottos along the walls of the wash—during rains, runoff from the mountains pours through these waterfalls into the washbed.

Your path crosses a fence line in the wash at 1.6 miles and then narrows through another bend in the wash. A mildly steep path—which was

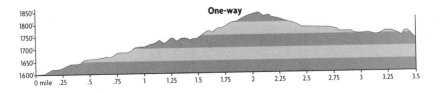

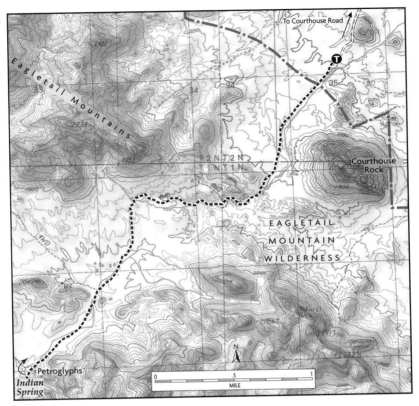

once a jeep road—heads northwest out of the wash, but your path is a gentle stroll again soon enough. You will zig west, then zag south again, and your trail is now running parallel to a ridgeline. You will roll easily in and out of several drainages, veering southwest—your heading for the remainder of the hike. Just past 2 miles, you cross a wide wash and then the faint trail exits the wash but remains parallel to it (keep the wash on your left). You join up with the wash at 2.75 miles, and this remains your path for the remainder of the hike. Listen for trilling rock wrens and watch out for speedy roadrunners as you and your dog make your way through the desert. By now, the Eagletails have obscured the giant monolith of Courthouse Rock from view.

You will see a small, rocky, flat-topped mesa on your left. Petroglyphs are found throughout this mesa, which is fairly easy to explore; on warmer

Opposite: Not close enough to Indian Spring

days, be especially alert for snakes. Please do not disturb the petroglyphs; they represent some of the best available evidence that this area was the site of some of the earliest Native American habitation in the Southwest and are an outstanding cultural resource.

You round the mesa's westernmost tip at 3.6 miles. Indian Spring is just a tad further along the path and nestled into more petroglyph-laden outcrops to your right—it is a cool treat for you and your dog if the spring happens to be flowing. Explore this area further if you like, or enjoy a shade break and when you are ready, head back the way you came.

Southern and Eastern Arizona

BORDER COUNTRY

57. Sycamore Canyon

Round trip: 5 miles
Hiking time: 3.5 hours
Difficulty: easy–moderate
High point: 4000 feet
Elevation gain: 200 feet
Best: late September through November; March through May
Map: Ruby USGS
Contact: Coronado National Forest, Nogales Ranger Station, (520) 281-2296
Note: Check rain runoff status before setting out. Due to the trail's proximity to the U.S.-Mexican border (and heavy patrols for various ongoing illegal activities in the region), hikers should exercise caution. Some portions of the route are through pools; your dog should be able to swim on this one.

Getting there: From Tucson, head south about 55 miles along Interstate 19. Before you get to Nogales and the border, exit at State Hwy 289 and take a right. This highway forks in 9 miles, where you will follow the sign to Arivaca (though you come nowhere close to that town), veering onto Forest Road 39 (left) at the fork. Continue on the well-graded dirt road

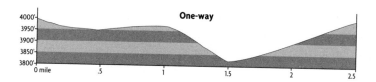

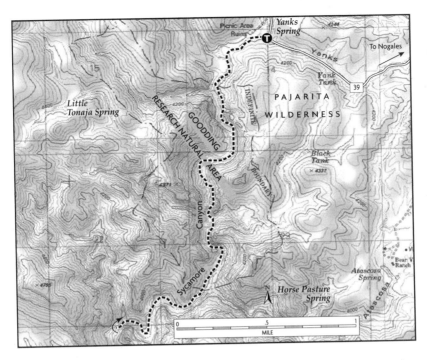

for another 9 miles—passenger cars will do fine on these roads. The turn into the trailhead for Sycamore Canyon Trail 40 is marked.

Ready to get your feet and paws wet? Sycamore Canyon is a gem of a hike in the desert Southwest because you and your dog will without a doubt get to romp through pools, wade (or swim) through deep cuts in the canyon, and generally revel in a cooling riverside outing. Fed by the perennial Sycamore Creek, Arizona sycamores, wild cassavas, and Goodding ash trees occur throughout the canyon, providing home sites, forage, and cover for all manner of wildlife, including the five-striped sparrow, mountain lions, javelinas, deer, coyotes, and rattlesnakes. The threatened Sonoran chub have a protected and enviable home in the creek's beautiful pools and backwaters. Nearly all of the trail is in the Pajarita Wilderness Area, and much of the first mile comprises part of the Goodding Research Natural Area.

Plan to pack in your water, or carry your water filter; ongoing cattle grazing in the area means you must treat any water you draw from the creek. On this hike you will also need midheight, water-compatible/waterproof hiking boots for traversing the stream through the canyon bottlenecks and

Time for a cooling dip.

unavoidable pools along your way. Make sure your dog is well conditioned and capable of swimming short distances before taking on this trail. If it's cool, pack a towel and Fido's vest to stave off hypothermia.

Once your dog is watered and leashed, proceed through the fairly open field past the Hank and Yank ruins—what remains is a portion of a wall from a homestead named for two brothers who originally settled in the area. Tall, leafy trees and canyon walls close in on the trail as you proceed. Though most dogs are not tempted to do so, see that your dog does not nibble on the maidenhair ferns—they can make her sick—heeding the leash rule makes good sense here. You will cross a wash before you lose sight of the trailhead, but soon enough you come upon your first of many ephemeral pools, moss-filled and cool on the paws.

Your path starts out heading south on an old jeep road toward the canyon. The only twists and turns you make along this trail follow the canyon and Sycamore Creek, always in a generally southward direction towards the U.S.-Mexico border. And what a ramble! Flanking the creek and side pools, gravelly beaches and cliff walls support islands of giant manzanitas, turpentine bushes, oaks, and junipers. The rocks themselves are alive with mosses, ferns, and lichens. The canyon walls and hilltops are craggy silhouettes of exposed volcanic rhyolite, shale, and sandstone conglomerates. As you make your way along drier stretches, the rocks click and shift, producing a sound reminiscent of the metallic clop of horses' hooves.

When it is time for you to wade (and for your dog to swim) through the first slot, or bottleneck, at just past the 0.5-mile mark, you are ready for a dip. Beyond this slot, the canyon remains fairly narrow for about 0.2 mile and more wading or boulder-hopping is necessary to proceed. The views on this remote hike—not to mention the muddy paws—are a great reward, however. The canyon widens again, allowing passage on the banks of the creek, walking through the shade cast by the cliff walls and the namesake sycamore trees that thrive here. The second major slot is your turnaround point, at just over 2.5 miles. The trail does go all the way to the border (another 3 miles), but take some time here for a splashy romp before exploring further or heading back the way you came.

58. Sonoita Creek

Round trip: 1.2 miles
Hiking time: 1 hour
Difficulty: easy
High point: 3881 feet
Elevation gain: 73 feet
Best: October through May
Map: Patagonia USGS
Contact: Patagonia Lake State Park (520) 287-6965, Sonoita Creek
    Natural Area Visitor Center, (520) 287-2791
Note: It is best to avoid this short trail when group activities are
    taking place—contact the visitor center for a schedule.

Getting there: Getting there is easy. From Tucson, take Interstate 10 southeast to State Hwy 83; then head south to Hwy 82. At Sonoita, which is 90

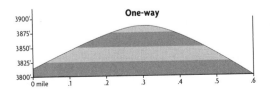

miles from Tucson, head southwest on Hwy 82 toward Patagonia; go 7 miles past Patagonia and turn right onto the Patagonia Lake State Park entrance road. Proceed to the fee station ($7.00 per vehicle is required), then enter the park and take the east (right) fork in the road and continue until the road loops around at the trailhead.

Patagonia Lake State Park is nestled between the rolling hills of the Patagonia and Santa Rita Mountains. It was the first major natural area designated by the state of Arizona, made possible by the damming of Sonoita Creek. Because the upstream wetlands remain largely undeveloped, this unique and beautiful area is enjoyed by the public year-round thanks to the state park which has grown up around the lake.

Like its cousin, the Nature Conservancy's Patagonia–Sonoita Creek Preserve (which does not allow dogs on trails), Sonoita Creek provides a striking example of native riparian habitats once common to southeastern Arizona. Fremont cottonwood–Goodding willow riparian forests shade the cienegas, or wetlands, that are fed by Sonoita Creek, one of the few remaining permanent streams in southeastern Arizona.

The Sonoita Creek watershed supports native fish and toads, and quenches the thirst of the region's mountain lion, bobcat, and white-tailed

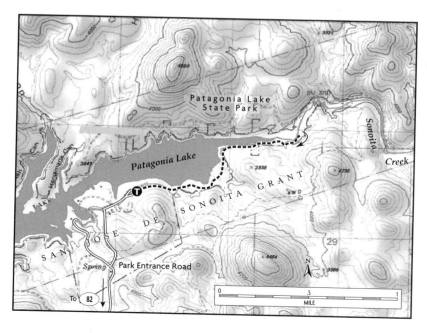

The placid Sonoita Creek flows into Patagonia Lake.

deer populations. Rattlesnakes are also commonly found in the area, particularly during the summer months. Follow the leash rules for the park and review first aid procedures for rattlesnake bite before setting out.

Once you and your dog are ready to hit the trail to the creek, double check that you have your binoculars. This is one of the richest birding areas in the Southwest. Blue herons often peek through the cattails on the shores of Patagonia Lake, but attentive avian enthusiasts hiking in May and September can also spot other native desert birds of wetlands: green kingfishers, northern beardless tyrannulers, violet crowned hummingbirds, and rose-throated becards.

This 1.2-mile trail is short and fairly level so hikers and dogs of all abilities can enjoy the shady path and mirror-image views of water and sky. Pack in your drinking water or pull from the creek at trail's end. (Remember to purify what you take since grazing still takes place directly upstream.)

Sonoita Creek Trail starts at an interpretive site detailing the wildlife and plants found in the region. Beyond this developed section, you descend to a forest path that winds in and out of dappled shade. A fork at 0.4 mile leads rightward into heavier forest cover; a good place to take out your binoculars and for your dog to enjoy a shadier stroll on warmer days. The trail soon departs from the trees and winds northward, finishing creekside at the 0.6-mile mark.

Sonoita Creek is a slow-moving and ever-changing watercourse that widens at the mouth of Patagonia Lake. It is sloshy going, so choose your footwear accordingly because the pretty area invites more exploration—and certainly some playtime! Your dog will love the muck, so a stop at one of the park's water facilities after the hike for a quick scrub of the paws will be the order of the day when you can bear to part with the creek and head back.

59. San Pedro River

Round trip: up to 20 miles
Hiking time: up to 9 hours
Difficulty: easy–moderate
High point: 4164 feet
Elevation change: 119 feet
Best: September through April
Maps: Hereford, Nicksville, Lewis Springs, and Fairbank USGS; Arizona Atlas and Gazetteer
Contact: Bureau of Land Management, Tucson Field Office, (520) 258-7200; and San Pedro Project Office, (520) 439-6400

Getting there: From Tucson, head east on Interstate 10 then south on State Hwy 90. In Sierra Vista, follow the signs to take Hwy 92 south; pass Hereford Road at Nicksville and follow Hwy 92 as it turns east past Ramsey Canyon (90 miles from Tucson). Continue on Hwy 92 east to another branch of Hereford Road, which you take left (north). Take a left into the Hereford Bridge trailhead—the bridge itself is closed, but the trailhead is accessible just beyond the road closure sign.

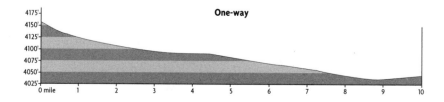

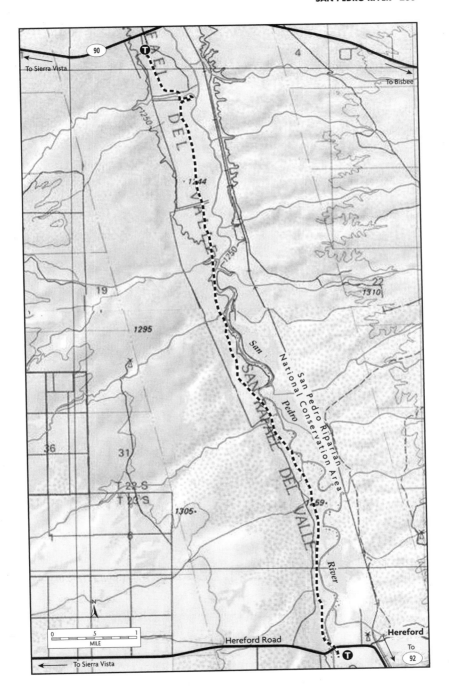

Note: To make a one-way, 10-mile trek, set up a shuttle with one car parked at the San Pedro House. Get there by staying on Hwy 90 through Sierra Vista and turning right at the San Pedro House trailhead; proceed in the second car to the Hereford Bridge trailhead by heading back west on Hwy 90, taking a left on Moson Road, a left at the dead end onto Hereford Road, a right onto Palominas, a left onto Hwy 92, a left onto yet another branch of Hereford Road, then a left into the Hereford Bridge trailhead. (The atlas suggested above will keep you on track.) Your convoluted drive around this washed-out bridge is well rewarded by having a more remote trailhead from which to begin your scenic day hike.

A plus for your dog on the San Pedro River hike is that no leashes are required except at the trailhead and at the San Pedro House terminus, provided your dog responds well to voice commands. Check with the BLM office before heading out about hunting activity in the area—hunting dogs, almost always off-leash, are allowed in the San Pedro Riparian National Conservation Area.

Once under way, you and your dog follow the contours of a shady river considered by naturalists and outdoor enthusiasts alike to be one of the world's unsung natural wonders. The trail lies almost entirely on the west side of the river, which means you must cross at the first convenient point, since Hereford Bridge trailhead starts you off on the east side of the San Pedro. Rain events can change the riverbed, but as of the time of this writing an easy crossing lies within 0.1 mile of the trailhead; you immediately find a faint footpath along the bank.

At various places on this hike, as along the first 0.3 mile, and especially if the river is running high, your path is—tantalizingly—just outside the cover of the Goodding willows and Fremont cottonwoods that are the cornerstone plants of this riparian ecosystem. Take heart: this hike is not recommended for summer, when the exposure and searing ambient temperatures would make hiking hazardous for your dog. In fact, the streambanks are well shaded and you have countless opportunities for easy access to shallow points on the river whenever your pooch needs a cooling dip. Do bring the drinking water you will need or plan to filter what you draw from the river, as grazing is permitted nearby.

As you and your dog amble north on this easy, downstream jaunt, you are in the thick of a massive migratory bird corridor: two to four million

Opposite: Checking Sparky's pads on a rest break along the San Pedro River (photo by Ken G. Sweat)

birds migrate here annually and more than 375 distinct species have been identified. This is an excellent place to take out your field glasses, but chances are you will glimpse great horned owls, Swainsons hawks, and American kestrels without optics.

Only the Costa Rican rain forest has a higher diversity of mammals than Cochise County, which encompasses the San Pedro Riparian National Conservation Area. Your dog's keen nose will probably lead you to the tracks and sign of raccoons, javelinas, deer, gophers, and that ubiquitous Arizona canid, the coyote.

Early fall is a particularly good time to enjoy this trail, when late-blooming wildflowers in the fields surrounding the river erupt with butterflies—more than 250 species at the latest count, including the western pygmy blue, queen, and mourning cloak butterflies.

A lovely and secluded beach at 8.8 miles makes for an excellent picnic spot—a great point for your last splash if you are doing the shuttle version of this hike, and a well-placed rest area if you are trekking the entire 20-mile round trip.

The last mile of the trail runs right into the San Pedro House interpretive loop at Kingfisher Pond. This is actually a former sand and gravel quarry that collects rainfall and makes a deep pool that would be a hazardous swimming hole, since its sheer sides prevent an easy exit. If your dog is a champion diver, be sure to keep her under control here. Since most of this interpretive path is quite busy on weekends, you should leash your dog here and keep her leashed as you head for your shuttle or if you need to use the comfort facilities. If you are hiking this trail round trip, head back the way you came whenever you and your dog are ready.

DRAGOON MOUNTAINS

60. Cochise Stronghold

Round trip: 6 miles
Hiking time: 3.5 hours
Difficulty: easy–moderate
High point: 6013 feet
Elevation gain: 1100 feet
Best: October through April
Map: Cochise Stronghold USGS
Contact: Coronado National Forest, Douglas Ranger Station,
  (520) 364-3468

Getting there: To get there from Tucson, take Interstate 10 east for 72 miles to US Hwy 191 and turn right (south). At Ironwood Road, watch for a sign directing you to turn right to Cochise Stronghold. Follow Ironwood all the way into the Cochise Campground, approximately 8 miles; the unpaved road is washboard, but accessible to passenger vehicles. The day fee at the campground is $5.00 per carload. No Mutt Mitts are provided here, so bring bags to pick up after your dog. Proceed to the back of the campground; the trailhead is located just next to a bridge.

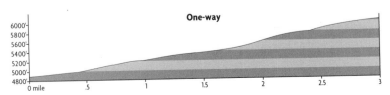

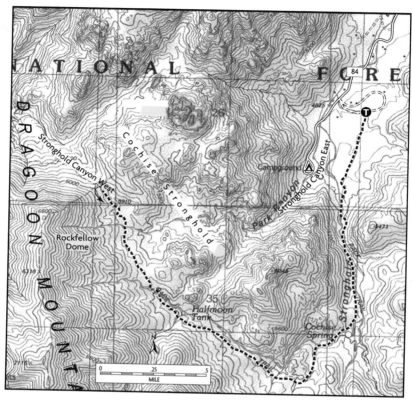

Once your dog is watered and leashed—remember to pack water in—cross the bridge to begin the Cochise Stronghold Trail 279. Though the pathway itself is very easy on boot and paw, with the exception of occasional rocky segments in the upper reaches, this trail takes you through the rugged natural fortress of the Chiricahua Apaches, a sanctuary for Cochise's troops in their bloody 12-year war with the U.S. Cavalry. (Cochise, legend has it, is buried somewhere in the stronghold.)

Once you cross the bridge, point the leash left. Before you get 0.25 mile in, the path begins climbing through an extravagantly lush, oak-juniper copse studded with turpentine bushes, blood-barked manzanitas, beargrass, Schott's yuccas, madrone trees, quinine bushes, agaves, and chilicates—a pepper plant. Stay alert and heed the leash rule, for deer, bears, and javelinas thrive in this bountiful place.

Opposite: Among the surreal hoodoos of the Cochise Stronghold

Your path overlooks a wash intersected at about 0.4 mile. At 0.5 mile, you will exit the wash to proceed through a gate and then cross a creek (often dry): the trail falls between the wash and the creekbed. A side trail heads left just before the 0.75-mile mark; stay to the right, heading uphill, for the Cochise Trail.

All along, your progress has been followed by the surreal hoodoos that populate the Dragoon Mountains. At 0.8 mile, you begin switchbacking up the path, now filling up with huge, flat boulders, and you find yourself among the hoodoos at last. These striking rock piles resemble whimsical sculptures whose gravity-defying stunts make a great diversion on this leg of the hike. Cochise Spring often bubbles up from the ground at 0.9 mile in a pretty, shaded area just perfect for a break; filter any water you take from this spring if it is running. Once you continue your climb toward the saddle, the path disappears into a creekbed for about 20 feet (waterproof boots are recommended for you after rains, but you won't hear Fido complain about her squelchy toes!); veer to the left and you will soon see a clear trail heading southwest. You are still in hoodoo-land for another 0.75 mile, with terrific views all around.

Right about the 2-mile mark, you come upon a well-shaded glade that secrets away Halfmoon Tank, a livestock watering hole. Your trail turns due west, then vaults uphill again to the northwest in the last approach to the saddle. As is the case on much of this hike, shade and comfortable rest spots are plentiful. From this vantage you can see Rockfellow Dome—a highly popular climbing spot. Raptors love these granite domes as well, so climbing is restricted (and therefore, hiking more solitary) from mid-February through June.

The stronghold divide, at just over 3 miles, is your turnaround point. Your view of the western Stronghold Canyon is a striking mosaic of greens, grays, and pinks. You and your dog can explore more, should paws be willing and tail still wagging—the trail continues another 1.75 miles into Stronghold Canyon West to Forest Road 687. When ready, simply turn the leash around and enjoy a saunter back the way you came.

SANTA RITA MOUNTAINS

61. Gardner Canyon

Round trip: 6 to 9 miles
Hiking time: 3.5 to 5 hours
Difficulty: difficult
High point: 8400 feet to 9453
Elevation change: 2330 to 3383 feet
Best: March through November
Map: Mt. Wrightson USGS
Contact: Coronado National Forest, Nogales Ranger Station, (520) 281-2296
Note: Check road conditions immediately after heavy rains and during spring snowmelt; several creek crossings on the drive are hazardous if flooding occurs.

Getting there: To get there from Tucson, take Interstate 10 east about 11 miles to the State Hwy 83 exit (south). Four miles before Sonoita, turn right (west) onto Gardner Canyon Road, also known as Forest Road 92. This unpaved road is rough in places; high clearance is a must and a four-wheel-drive vehicle is recommended. Keep left at the fork with FR 163. When you see the sign for Apache Springs Ranch, take the rightward fork. After your first crossing of Cave Creek—the creek often spills over this unmaintained road—there is a signed intersection; turn left

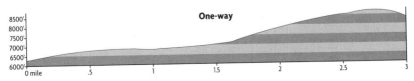

One-way

onto FR 785 and proceed 4 miles to the trailhead. Let your dog have a go at her water bowl, leash her up, pack bags and plenty of drinking water, and you are ready for the Mt. Wrightson Wilderness Area.

This remote route to Mt. Wrightson's upper reaches lifts off humbly, beside a quiet, perennial stream, heading southwest. The effusive lushness that springs from the marriage of shade and water in southwestern canyons produces a convivial jumble of plant life: agaves, yuccas, barrel cacti, prickly pear cacti, bear grass, rose mallows, penstemons, woodsorrels, sages, cat-claw bushes, Arizona cypress, alligator and one-seed junipers, and ponderosa pines. Snakes—including rattlesnakes—inhabit the area as well, so stay alert. If you are very lucky, you might spot a coati or some white-tailed deer foraging at the streamside.

For a short time, you and your dog crisscross this drainage (waterproof hiking boots are a big plus in spring and late summer). You have a comfortable walking surface when you begin your climb away from this riparian madrean woodland. Your path zigs southwest, then zags south, switchbacking uphill to lead you through both the dappled light of an open ponderosa pine forest and through sunlit, open parks. You top out at 1.2 miles on a ridge, where there is a trail junction: the Walker Basin Trail veers left and the Gardner Trail 143 continues straight, through the clearing. You stay relatively well shaded on this steeper segment. Alongside the switchbacking path, a number of dispersed campsites make excellent rest areas if you and your dog need to catch your breath or have a drink. At 2.5 miles, you traverse a level

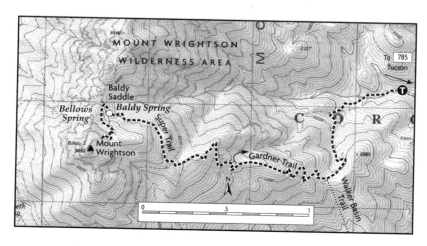

From cacti to pines and coati to songbirds, the Gardner Canyon Trail offers a delightful study in contrasts for you and your dog to explore and enjoy.

section of the forest with pretty boulders dotted throughout—another terrific spot for a break or picnic now or on your way out.

At 2.75 miles, you begin your last short vault uphill to the end of the Gardner Canyon Trail at the junction with the Super Trail, having gained 2300 feet elevation so far. This is the terminus. Enjoy approaching the Wrightson summit by hiking the entire length of the Super Trail (see Hike 62). You can approach the summit more directly from here if your water supplies are good and your dog's tail is still wagging. Simply go north (right) and uphill on the Super Trail past Baldy Spring to Baldy Saddle. Turn left (south) on the Crest Trail to take in the superb views from Mt. Wrightson, the tallest point in the Santa Rita Mountains. Summitting adds just over 3 miles (round trip) and 1050 feet of elevation gain to the hike. Almost all of the last 0.25 mile is exposed; be sure you have packed enough water, since Baldy Spring is unreliable during dry months.

When you are ready, point the leash downhill and return the way you came, allowing time for you and your dog to get a good long splash break when you hit the stream at the bottom of Gardner Canyon.

62. Super

Round trip: 13 to 16 miles
Hiking time: 6 to 8 hours
Difficulty: difficult
High point: 9453
Elevation gain: 4053
Best: March through November
Maps: Mt. Hopkins and Mt. Wrightson USGS
Contact: Coronado National Forest, Nogales Ranger Station,
  (520) 281-2296

Getting there: From Tucson, head south on Interstate 19 about 25 miles
to Continental Road, exit 63. Go left (east) and proceed 1.2 miles to the
Madera Canyon turnoff. This road leads directly to the Madera Canyon
Recreation Area; use any self-serve station to pay the day use fee ($5.00
per vehicle) and continue driving until the road ends at the trailhead.
Arrive early because the parking lot is small and this trailhead serves
several hiking trails.

Once your dog is watered and leashed, take the Super Trail 134 southeast from the parking area. Your path initially lies under the shade of a
cool oak and mixed-pine forest; however, there are large sections of this
trail that are exposed. Watch summer temperatures carefully while planning your trip, and even on the mildest days, bring more water than you
think you need. Super is a "super" steep trail in places; you will gain 4000
feet in 13 miles. What you and your dog will enjoy about this longer,
drier route is that it is almost entirely within the Mt. Wrightson Wilderness Area and is much less crowded than the Old Baldy Trail.

  The first notable stop for you and your pooch is Sprung Spring (3.6
miles), a pretty, high-elevation oasis just below Josephine Saddle, about

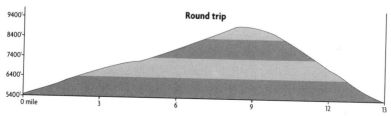

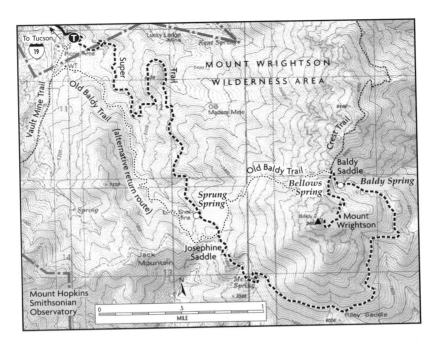

halfway up the craggy summit of Mt. Wrightson. To get there, you will climb a ridge and cross a wash; the climb is gentle and the path is paw-friendly here. The trail winds north, then makes a wide turn to the south. Along this segment, you have excellent views of the Mt. Hopkins Smithsonian Observatory. Closer in, note the bear grass, yuccas, turpentine bushes, and tiny resurrection ferns, tightly tucked into rock crevices, that are common throughout Madera Canyon. This is a world-renowned birding area, so double-check that you have your binoculars and camera before you head out. You cannot miss Sprung Spring—it is fairly reliable and the surrounds are lush, lush, lush. Purify what you take to drink and pick a shady spot to enjoy a water break with your dog while listening to the chatter of birds.

When you have enough of the oasis vibe, keep trekking south a short distance. At Josephine Saddle, turn northeast, pass the Temporal Gulch Trail junction, and take a right at the next junction to follow the Super Trail as it swings around the south side of Mt. Wrightson's summit. Continue heading up the gentle rise of this high desert segment of the Super Trail, past the Gardner Canyon Trail terminus (6.2 miles), and onto Baldy Saddle. The trail passes Baldy Spring, but plan to break out your own stores since it is rarely more than a trickle. At the saddle at 7.2 miles, you turn south onto the Crest Trail to ascend the summit along a series of switchbacks. Once past the cool pines, enjoy the panoramic views, which stretch more than 50 miles in all directions; when you are ready for shade turn the leash around and head out the way you came.

If you want a shorter and even shadier return route—a good option on warmer days if the trail is not too crowded—take the Old Baldy path to the left (west) at the junction with the Crest and Super Trails. On this steeper, rockier path, water is usually scarce, but you can break out the water bottles and your dog's water bowl at any number of shady spots whenever your dog needs a drink. At about 4.7 miles from the summit, the Old Baldy Trail turns southwest and in no time joins up with the Vault Mine Trail—a moderately steep path. Take Vault Mine Trail right (northeast) for 0.3 mile to return to the trailhead.

Boulders along the Super Trail demonstrate a generous live-and-let-live philosophy by yielding their meager moisture to lichens, ferns, and mosses.

SANTA CATALINA MOUNTAINS AND AREA

63. Romero Canyon to Montrose Pools

Round trip: 2 miles
Hiking time: 1 hour
Difficulty: easy
High point: 3100 feet
Elevation gain: 377 feet
Best: October through May
Map: Oro Valley USGS
Contact: Catalina State Park Ranger Station, (520) 628-5798

Getting there: Travel to Catalina State Park is a breeze. From Tucson, head north approximately 9 miles on Oracle Road and turn east into the park. The day use fee is $6.00 per vehicle; from the fee station, proceed down the park drive, which ends at the trailhead for Romero Canyon Trail 8.

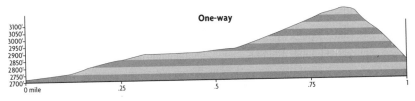

This short, desert upland hike is scenic—and exposed. Pack in water and water your dog well before leashing her and heading out. The trail is well traveled on weekends during the recommended seasons—following leash and waste pickup regulations is not just good for this desert environment (and for your dog), it is a courtesy to other trail users.

Once you cross the park drive to approach the trailhead, follow the sign to join up with the Romero Canyon Trail. You and your dog strike boot and paw onto a wide, sandy path that crosses the Sutherland Wash and then vaults uphill for 0.2 mile—in fact, much of your elevation change on this hike is in this initial climb. Breathtaking views of Romero Pass and the sky islands of the Santa Catalina Mountains reward your ascent. You are peering into part of the Pusch Ridge Wilderness, established in 1978, which encompasses Sonoran Desert, semidesert grassland, oak woodland, chaparral, ponderosa pine, and mixed conifer ecosystems.

Closer in, the setting is just as striking. On this hike, you and your dog enjoy an incredibly diverse desert upland. If you see an insect impaled on a cholla spine, you have found a temporary feeding ground for the loggerhead shrike, a songbird also known as the butcher bird, which uses this method to store food. If the desert mistletoe has berries, the cardinal-like phainopepla will not be far away.

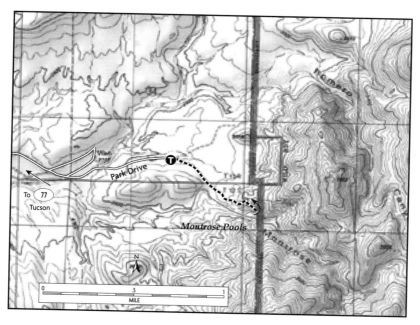

Romero Canyon is a defiant landscape.

The remainder of the trail is, to the 1-mile mark, a straight, steady ascent to the Catalina State Park–Coronado National Forest boundary. At the Romero Canyon–Montrose Canyon fork, a picnic bench and an overlook to your right yield a lovely view of the canyon and pools below. While the path down to the pools is not an official park or Forest Service trail, there is no prohibition against using it. Consider your and your dog's physical condition before descending this short scramble down to the pools, where the cliffs cast some shade and if it has rained recently, you can enjoy a splash break before turning back the way you came.

64. Sutherland

Round trip: 5.2 miles
Hiking time: 3 hours
Difficulty: easy
High point: 3525 feet
Elevation gain: 650 feet
Best: October through May
Map: Oro Valley USGS
Contact: Catalina State Park Ranger Station, (520) 628-5798

Getting there: From Tucson, take Oracle Road north approximately 9 miles and turn east into the park. Day use fee is $6.00 per vehicle; from

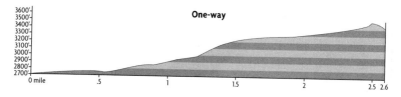

the fee station, proceed down the park drive, which ends at the trailhead for Sutherland Trail 6.

The best time to travel to the foothills of the Santa Catalinas depends on your interest—wildflowers dazzle the eyes from March through May, and fall, spring, and winter offer spectacular opportunities to view (and hear) up to 140 species of permanent and migrating birds. Of course the mountain views make for a lovely hike at any time. The trail is especially nice after rains or snowmelt; gurgling washes ensure ample opportunity for cooling breaks.

Once your dog is watered and leashed—remember to pack in water for the hike or plan to treat water you take from the ephemeral streams you encounter along the way—cross the park road and follow the signpost onto a leftward path, which directs you to the Sutherland junction. Here, take a right onto the Sutherland Trail. You begin your hike on a wide, sandy gravel path which meanders through an old-growth mesquite *bosque* (riparian forest) as it loosely follows Sutherland Wash toward the Santa Catalina Mountains. To your left is a slightly elevated ridge, where a chorus line of saguaros rises up from behind the mesquites, their already impressive heights exaggerated by their high perch.

You emerge from the mesquite *bosque* at about 0.3 mile and from here the trail is mostly exposed. At 0.3 and 0.4 mile, you cross Sutherland Wash, which will require some easy boulder-hopping or wading if any water is flowing—this cooling dip will feel terrific to your dog, especially on the way out. Before you reach 0.6 mile a marked fork points you right to continue on the Sutherland Trail. After an easy jaunt for a little over 0.1 mile, you descend to another section of the wash and another signed fork: stay left to continue on the Sutherland Trail. Shortly you will make two moderate ascents onto a ridge and climb away from the wash system.

Though you are still in mesquite country, your trek into the Santa Catalina foothills takes you through a mixed desert upland terrain dotted with stands of prickly pear cacti, palo verde trees, saguaro cacti, barrel cacti, yuccas, agaves, ocotillos, and mormon tea (joint fir). Fascinating rock formations greet your every turn of the trail; knobby plant roots claw, bird-like, at the impressionistic boulders, which sport speckles of purple, orange, and black.

In fact, throughout the remaining 1.25 miles of the hike, huge boulder fields dominate the landscape (very little boulder-hopping is required on this well-maintained park trail, however). Green, springy mosses and ferns peek out from between the desert pavement and rock overhangs, producing a slight shock to the eyes and a welcome reminder of what magic such little water and shade can do in a desert. Along your way here, tabletop rocks and piles of boulders offer some shade, and you will want to take advantage of these spots to give your dog a welcome water break. One note of caution—in warmer weather, this area is a haven for snakes, so keep a firm grip on the leash and make sure that hands, noses, and paws stay out of crevices!

You will come to a gate and the Catalina State Park boundary at about 2.5 miles. Go through the gate, close it after you, and drop down to a wash, about 25 yards along the trail. If the water is flowing, explore this pretty creekside area: there are several excellent spots for a rest and splash break before turning around and heading out the way you came. Note

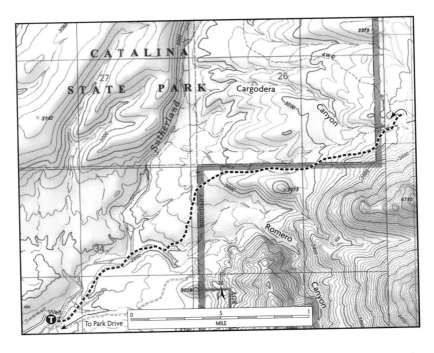

A desert wash still trickling after rains along the Sutherland Trail

that though the Sutherland Trail continues for another 7.5 miles, this is the turnaround point for hiking with dogs—the upper portion of the trail crosses through a restricted desert bighorn sheep management area and no dogs are allowed.

65. Butterfly to Crystal Spring

Round trip: 7.3 miles
Hiking time: 4 hours
Difficulty: moderate–difficult
High point: 7737 feet
Elevation change: 1277 feet
Best: March through November
Map: Mt. Bigelow USGS
Contact: Coronado National Forest, Santa Catalina Ranger Station, (520) 749-8700

Getting there: To get to this scenic Mt. Lemmon Trail, take Tanque Verde Road in Tucson and in just over 3 miles merge onto the Catalina Highway heading northeast. At the Coronado National Forest boundary, you must pay for a day pass, which currently is $5.00 per vehicle. Continue on Catalina—also called Mt. Lemmon Road—to just shy of 3 miles past the Palisades Visitor Center. On your right, there is a parking lot for the Butterfly Trail 16. Once your dog is watered and leashed, you are ready for your hike—remember to pack in water, and be sure to filter any water you drink from the spring.

The trail starts out on an old road and gently loses elevation as you head into the pine-oak forest; eventually you will lose 1200 feet. You leave pavement behind in just 200 feet; shortly there is a fork, where you should veer left. At 0.2 mile, point the leash leftward down some stone steps and onto a narrow, compacted earth path. You descend more rapidly through the cool ponderosas here. Occasionally, as you make your way east and north around Butterfly Peak, the tree canopy parts enough for you to enjoy spectacular vistas of Alder Canyon and the San Pedro Valley. The pretty scenery pops up again and again as you traverse more exposed ridgelines (or the occasional fire-scorched area) and as the pines temporarily give way to less statuesque madrones, maples, oaks, and alligator junipers.

   The path carries you and your dog through several narrow ravines where the footing is tricky—use extra caution if it has rained recently. In wetter years, you will see columbines and butterfly weed poking out from between the boulders along the trail. And as the trail's name suggests, a butterfly field guide is a good read before you head out. The Southwest is home to more than half of North American butterfly species and the Santa Catalina range is one of the best viewing spots in the Southwest. Plan to take your hike in spring or between summer rains (July to August), and then while you are taking a shade break with your pooch, you can enjoy the flits and flurries of these colorful creatures.

   At 0.9 mile, the trail makes steeper switchbacks downhill but the heading is still eastward. The Crystal Spring Trail 17 turnoff comes at 1.4 miles and leads you and your dog north along a more exposed

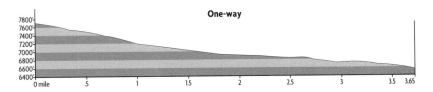

ridgeline. A particularly impressive alligator juniper beckons a shady rest and water break at the 1.9-mile mark, but it is not long before you and your dog are trekking through the shade again. You turn southwest as the trail starts crossing wash after wash—you and your dog are walking through the mountain's shallow folds. During snowmelt or after rains, this hike is a real joy for dogs. Occasionally, the path fades—when this happens at 2.2 miles, continue your southwesterly heading and you will pick up the trail again. From this point, the trail is very easy to discern as it winds its way down and eventually northwest along the last stretch toward the spring.

Crystal Spring is to the left of the trail just past 3.6 miles; it pours from beneath a walnut tree and feeds the flat, grassy area all around this section of the trail. Fairly reliable except in the driest times, it is easy to find. (Before you get to the spring, there is a very old walnut tree that has "swallowed" a Forest Service sign—it is difficult to catch this, but if you spot it you will know that you are within about 40 feet of the spring.) If the spring is running, let your dog muddy her paws again before turning the leash around heading out the way you came.

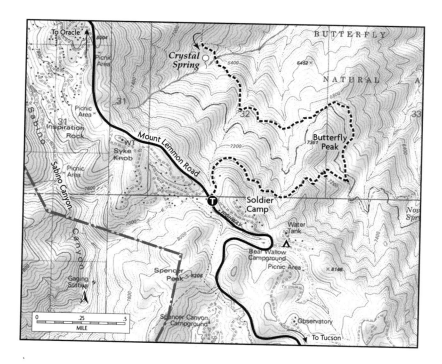

Artemis uses her rest break to catch a power nap.

66. Green Mountain to Maverick Spring

Round trip: 4.6 miles
Hiking time: 3 hours
Difficulty: moderate
High point: 7314 feet
Elevation change: 797 feet
Best: March through November
Map: Mt. Bigelow USGS
Contact: Coronado National Forest, Santa Catalina Ranger Station, (520) 749-8700

Getting there: To get there from the Tucson intersection of Grant/Kolb Road and Tanque Verde, take Tanque Verde east for just over 3 miles,

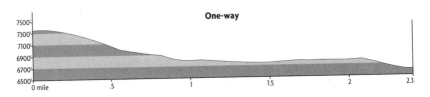

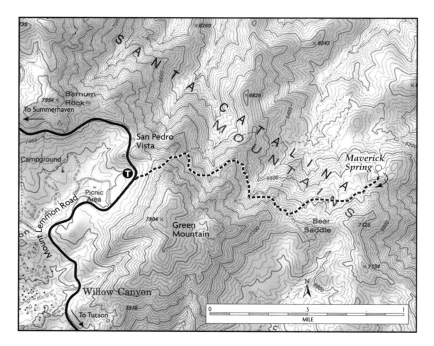

and follow the signs onto the Catalina Highway. Proceed approximately 5 miles to the Coronado National Forest fee station—a $5.00 day use fee per vehicle is required. Continue on the scenic Catalina Highway, which is also Mt. Lemmon Road, past mile marker 17 and 0.3 mile past Rose Canyon Road (which is on your left). Parking for the Green Mountain Trail 21 is on your right. This is a newly constructed trailhead—the old San Pedro Vista trailhead for Green Mountain has been closed. If you come to the San Pedro Vista, you have gone 0.1 mile too far.

Cool ponderosa pines, chaparral-oak woodlands, and a flowing spring at trail's end—this path through the visually stunning Santa Catalina Mountains is a varied and sometimes challenging romp for two- and four-legged hikers alike.

After just a 0.2-mile climb from the trailhead, the San Pedro Vista floats up into view. Keep your "wows" handy because the winding forest path along the mini-skirt line of Green Mountain offers many views of the Santa Catalinas. The views draw other visitors as well, particularly during the spring and autumn, so follow the leash rules and let your dog enjoy the trail close at heel.

At the junction for the Brush Corral and Green Mountain Trails, continue southeast on the Green Mountain Trail to reach Maverick Spring. Just past this 0.3-mile mark, you begin to see scars left by the Bullock fire. Ghost trees mark the fire's path and these remnants, or snags, provide perches for Cooper's hawks. The bark that sloughs from fire-damaged trees makes a charcoal, saffron, and umber mosaic on the trail floor in places.

As a practical matter, the fire consumed some of the shade along the trail. Additionally, the next 0.7 mile of trail drops onto lower cliffs and into oak-chaparral territory, which means you and your dog are hiking on more exposed terrain that is certainly hotter and drier than that on the rest of the hike. Pay special attention to your dog's progress on warmer days—even mild dehydration is a serious issue for canines. Be sure you bring plenty of water and plan to purify any that you get at the spring to supplement your stores.

Just before the Maverick Spring Trail 704 turnoff (1.8 miles), you have already started to climb back into ponderosa pine territory. You will encounter steep switchbacks through a bouldery area—just follow the cliff line and you will not lose the trail.

At 1.9 miles, head northeast toward the spring along a downhill track. Follow cairn markings to cross the ephemeral washes. At 2.2 miles, the trail gets a little sketchy—your northeasterly heading on this segment of trail is constant, so you'll pick up the path in a bit.

Hardy autumn blooms grace the trail to Maverick Spring.

When you come upon Maverick Spring, it will be difficult not to compare it to a Tolkien-esque, fantasy glade. The spring is on a steep slope and even in the driest of seasons there is almost always water in the wildlife watering hole about 25 yards downhill. You will want to take some time here and soak up the cool, lush vibe of Maverick Spring—the way you came is a workout on the return leg. Make sure to keep a few trail treats back at your vehicle to reward your dog at the end of this pleasant day hike.

67. Arizona Trail to High Jinks

Round trip: 3.8 miles
Hiking time: 2.5 hours
Difficulty: easy
High point: 5046 feet
Elevation gain: 647 feet
Best: October through May
Maps: Oracle and Campo Bonito USGS
Contact: Coronado National Forest, Santa Catalina Ranger Station, (520) 749-8700

Getting there: To get to the trailhead, take State Hwy 77 north then east from Tucson. Proceed about 30 miles on Hwy 77, also known as Oracle Road, to the Oracle turnoff at American Avenue, and head east. Take a right on Mt. Lemmon Road and go past the Oracle State Park entrance. Once the pavement ends, you take a rightward fork to continue on Mt. Lemmon Road towards the youth camp, which is signed. Though it is a rough dirt road, high-clearance or four-wheel-drive vehicles are not necessary. The trailhead is on your right at the corral.

This pretty route on part of the Santa Catalina section of the Arizona Trail offers a shorter alternative to the Oracle segment day hike (see Hike 69),

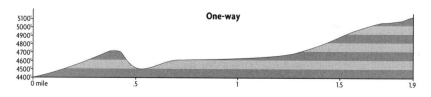

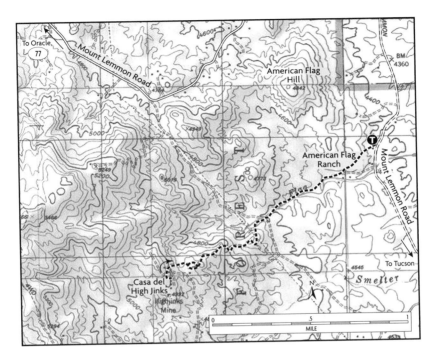

in case you and your dog only have just so much quality tail-wagging time to spend on the trail. Even though it is a short hike, plan to pack in plenty of water since a fair proportion of the trail is fully exposed. (As in all fragile desert environments, pack out all waste.)

Once your dog is watered and leashed, you pass through the rustic arch at the trailhead and ascend a low, lush hill. The loose and rocky switchbacks are closely lined with agave, prickly pear, manzanita, and cane cholla—if you look carefully at the desert pavement, you will also find tiny clumps of mammalaria and hedgehog cacti peeking out from under their shrubby nurse plants.

You top the hill and the Santa Catalina Mountains greet you in style. The trail continues with several long switchbacks to an ephemeral wash that is as pleasant as it is shady: junipers and oaks spring from the very rocks. The path becomes sandy as you traverse the wash here. You cross the wash twice at 0.5 mile. Recent flooding has washed part of the trail away at this point; simply continue your south-southwest heading and you will pick up the trail within 50 feet. You continue following the wash system through the 0.6-mile mark and make one more crossing—this is a good time for a splashy romp if there has been a recent rain or snowmelt.

From here, the trail leaves the wash. At 0.75 mile you climb another small hill before ascending to the next rocky promontory in what appears now to be a sea of boulders. Keep your binoculars handy for some excellent birdwatching along this stretch, but you may not need them: birds here seem completely nonplussed, rarely flitting more than one mesquite tree away from their perches as you and your dog make your way.

At 1 mile, the trail forms a T at an old road, which you follow to the northwest (right) for about 15 feet. You will see a marker directing you onto a path to your left and up another hill. Meet another road at 1.1 miles; follow the trail marker to the right. This section of trail shows evidence of a recent fire. You will see that some of the charred shrubs—especially the woody manzanitas—are already crown-sprouting: tender, bright-green leaves offer promise to a swath of what is essentially standing ash.

As you continue your long, moderate ascent among ever-higher hills, beautiful rock forms steal the scene. Beginning at about 1.4 miles, there are a number of places that offer both shade and stunning views. You round a particularly impressive hill at 1.6 miles, and a loop path runs all

A woodland scarred by fire

the way around it. Behind the hill, you see another road. Proceed up the road to the right and stop in at La Casa del High Jinks, which is on the National Register of Historic Places. On site is a buckboard wagon used by Elizabeth Taylor and Tom Skerrit in "Poker Alice," which was filmed in nearby Tucson. Buffalo Bill Cody once staked the High Jinks gold mine and lived and entertained at a cabin here until 1917. The beautifully restored buildings are a delightful setting for a water break before heading back the way you came.

68. Mariposa

Round trip: 3 miles
Hiking time: 2 hours
Difficulty: easy
High point: 4372 feet
Elevation gain: 67 feet
Best: October through May
Map: North of Oracle USGS
Contact: Oracle State Park, (520) 896-2425

Getting there: To get to the trailhead, take State Hwy 77 north then east from Tucson. Proceed about 30 miles on Hwy 77, also known as Oracle Road, to the Oracle turnoff at American Avenue, and turn right. Drive 2.3 miles and turn right onto Mt. Lemmon Road. Proceed to the Oracle State Park entrance road, which is posted, and take a left into the park. Past the fee station (day use fee is $6.00 per vehicle), continue on the entrance road to the Oak Woodland parking area on your right. The Mariposa trailhead is directly north, across the entrance road from the parking area.

The hills in Oracle State Park's grassy oak- and mesquite-dotted landscape beckon hikers to take to the trails and enjoy spectacular desert

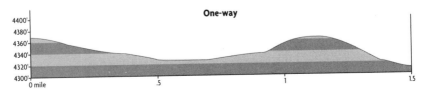

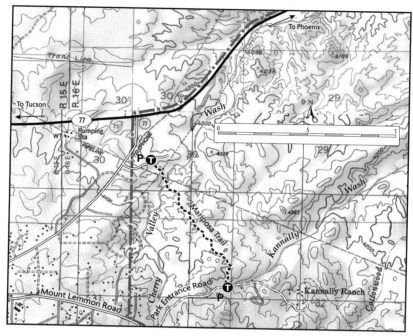

and mountain panoramas. The Mariposa and Arizona Trail segments are two of the very few trails within Oracle State Park on which your leashed dog can accompany you. Be sure to bring bags to pick up dog waste, since burying is inappropriate in this environment and no trash facilities are provided. Your dog will be glad you took her along because the slightly higher elevation and light shade from desert trees means that this trail is a bit cooler on the pads. Bring adequate water, though, since there is rarely water available in the washes for cooling off.

Your dog will enjoy winding in and out of the shade of the scrubby oak and mesquite trees that dot this landscape: just let the hills and washes roll under your feet and paws along the easy, 1.5-mile Mariposa Trail.

Only 0.2 mile after you set out, your gentle ascent northward is rewarded with terrific views to the east of the Santa Catalina Mountains. The well-maintained, rocky trail dips and then rises further into the boulder-studded hills. The path skirts closely enough around these scenic rock formations that you and Fido can touch (and sniff) them.

The trail descends into a shady wash at the 0.4-mile mark, but soon you are back to the hills. It is a testament to how flat this landscape is that the small climbs on this hike offer such sweeping views of the park,

Sparky and Ken enjoy a shady water break along the Mariposa Trail.

the town of Oracle, and the surrounding desert. Once you and your dog dip down again onto the plains and lower hills, the trail feels remote once more.

At 1.4 miles, you and your dog approach the Cherry Valley Wash parking area. There is a junction here which provides a link to the Arizona Trail segment through Oracle State Park. Check your water supply and see if your dog's tail is still wagging. If so, you can extend the hike from here (see Hike 69, Arizona Trail at Oracle)—or head back the way you came.

69. Arizona Trail at Oracle

Round trip: 7.6 miles
Hiking time: 4 hours
Difficulty: easy–moderate
High point: 4243 feet
Elevation gain: 418 feet
Best: October through May
Map: North of Oracle USGS
Contact: Oracle State Park, (520) 896-2425

Getting there: To get there from Tucson, head north and then east on Hwy 77. Continue about 30 miles on Hwy 77, also know as Oracle Road, until the Oracle turnoff at American Avenue, and turn right. Continue on American Avenue past the Mt. Lemmon Road/Oracle State Park turnoff and park at the Cherry Valley entrance (on your right). A day use fee of $6.00 per carload is required and a self-serve pay station is available.

Plan to take plenty of water on this hike—shade is plentiful through and along the typically dry washbeds, but the path along ridgelines is largely exposed. Once your dog is leashed, you are ready for the Arizona Trail loop.

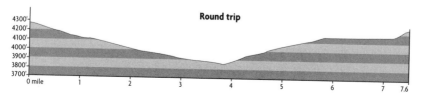

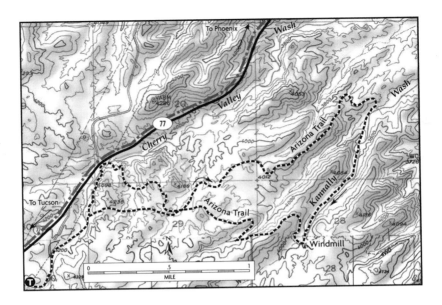

Your loop through the Oracle State Park segment of the Arizona Trail follows multi-user paths that approach the foothills of the scenic Santa Catalina Mountains. The park's plains and woodlands were once used by the Hohokam. The Kannally family, who established a ranch here at the beginning of the twentieth century, left the land to Defenders of Wildlife in 1976, who then transferred the property to the Arizona State Parks Board, which created Oracle State Park Center for Environmental Education. The Arizona Trail is a nearly completed statewide trail system, open to all nonmotorized uses (and canines!), that spans from Mexico to Utah. This segment of the Arizona Trail is a fairly recent addition to Oracle State Park.

From the trailhead, take the path leading straight ahead and downhill to Cherry Valley Wash. Once you have entered the wash at just under the 0.2-mile mark, take a left.

This first leg of your loop hike proceeds under the welcome cover of mesquites, junipers, and oak trees on a trail that alternates between a somewhat rocky, terra-cotta footpath to the finely decomposed desert pavement in the wash. While the trail is remarkably clear of debris, keep an eye out for the odd prickly pear pad or cholla bud that has "strayed" from the parent plant and plopped onto the path.

At 0.7 mile, you will see a rightward path that is your return route—

Cane cholla along the Arizona Trail

continue straight (northeast) and follow the trail as it turns southeast in a little more than 0.5 mile. You ascend a ridgeline and have a gorgeous view of the rolling hills in this classic desert upland: pretty outcroppings studded with cacti, yuccas, and manzanitas jut out above the mesquite- and oak-lined lowlands.

At just over 2 miles, the trail takes a sharp northeast turn into the Kannally Wash basin and for the next 3 miles, you are rolling in and through ridges and washbeds. Plenty of shady spots are available for water breaks along the way, which will keep your pooch's tail wagging throughout this hike. At the 3.6-mile mark, your trail swings southward again towards the windmill (at 5 miles), where you then turn west. Saunter along gentle switchbacks through the hills for the next 1.8 miles before turning southwest to take Cherry Valley Wash back to the trailhead. There are many points along the wash trail suitable for a last water-and-treat break or a picnic before putting paw and boot back on the pavement and heading home.

70. Ironwood Forest National Monument

Round trip: 1.4 miles
Hiking time: 1 hour
Difficulty: easy
High point: 2348 feet
Elevation gain: 60 feet
Best: October through May
Map: Silverbell East USGS
Contact: Bureau of Land Management, Tucson Field Office,
(520) 258-7200

Getting there: Drive approximately 19 miles northwest from Tucson on Interstate 10, take the Marana exit 236 west, and check your odometer. At the first stop sign, Trico-Marana Road, take a right. Stay on this road as it winds west-southwest; you will cross the Santa Cruz River. At 6.3 miles you come to an intersection with Silverbell Road; head northwest (right) here. At 14 miles, the pavement ends. At 14.3 miles you veer right at an unmarked fork to continue on Silverbell. You will cross a gas pipeline road at 16.9 miles. From the gas pipeline road, continue on Silverbell for 2.8 miles (to your 19.7-mile mark) and veer left at an unmarked fork. Continue south on this unmaintained segment of Silverbell (a high-clearance vehicle is a must) until the road forks again in 1.2 miles (the 20.9-mile mark). Head right and uphill here, veer left at the water tank, and in 0.75 mile, at the 21.6 mile mark, park to the right next to the gate. This is your trailhead.

The stunning scenery, wildlife values, and archaeological interest in the Ironwood Forest National Monument make this primitive recreation area a terrific cool-weather hike with your dog. You will need to pack in water, as washes tend to be dry except immediately after rains; pack out all waste. And be especially alert on warm days—four types of rattlesnakes

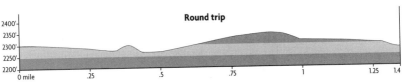

call this pristine desert upland home. Review snakebite first-aid procedures and keep hands, paws, and noses away from rock overhangs and any other places where vision is restricted. Because this is a desert bighorn sheep management area, leashes are required in the monument; once your dog is watered and leashed, you are ready to go.

Your trailhead is on the north side of Ragged Top. From the parking area, head left through the gate—close it behind you—and follow what used to be a mine road. In less than 0.1 mile, you pass through carefully placed boulders which mark an accessible path into the wash that comprises part of your route. You will take a left, heading initially southeast along the wash bottom.

Thanks to the dense vegetation, fairly high walls, and jutting, tumbled outcroppings, your path is often well shaded. The washbed is a combination of sand and slickrock—fine on paw and boot. In fact, boots of at least midheight are recommended so that you do not load up your shoes with sand—the ankle support is also helpful on your scrambles in and out of the wash, and on your brief overland trek.

The caliche, or lime-based beds, along the walls of the wash and throughout Ragged Top's peaks and saddles are prime desert tortoise habitat; chuckwallas and Gila monsters dart in and among the boulders here

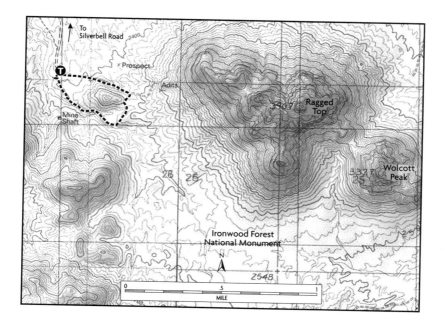

Petroglyphs near Ragged Top

too. Lest you wonder whether humans and canines ought to be interloping on what seems a reptilian paradise, look to your left just before the 0.2-mile mark. The petroglyphs here are a sign that this area has drawn visitors and sustained human populations—and their domesticated animals, surely—for many centuries.

At just past the 0.5-mile point, you will exit the wash using a convenient outcropping on your left, heading northeast. It is a scramble and small dogs may need some assistance. Once you make it past the lip of the wash, you travel overland to the top of the ridge, due north. Lush stands of ironwoods, saguaros, palo verde and mesquite trees, creosote bushes, and all manner of small cacti crowd the landscape. You have a great view of Ragged Top to your front and right, and now is a good time to break out your field glasses in case desert bighorn are on the ramble. When you top out at the ridge, take time for a water break and to enjoy more rock art and wildlife viewing.

From the ridge, make your way overland toward another old mining road. You will cross two small washes, around the 0.7-mile mark, on your generally northward heading. Just as you exit the first wash, you will see an old exploratory mining pit to your right fitted with modern bat grates. The grates keep people and dogs from falling in but allow bats who have reclaimed these pits to safely pass through.

At 0.75 mile, you will need to briefly zig northwest for easier travel, then shortly zag due north to catch up to the jeep trail—another old mining road—which becomes your path at the 0.8 mile mark. Enjoy the stunning view to the northwest of an amazingly dense forest of saguaros: in this section of the monument, saguaro density is even higher than in Saguaro National Park. In fact, ironwood trees are excellent nurse plants for young saguaro cacti, offering shade and protection against trampling from two-and four-legged creatures happening by. Magnificent and hardy, ironwoods can live up to 800 years. This monument represents one of the riches stands in the Sonoran Desert. Watch late spring temperatures carefully because late May is when both ironwoods and saguaros bloom— if it is not too hot, this is an excellent time to watch bats flit in the evening sky and pollinate the waxy white flowers crowning the saguaros.

Water supply and climate permitting, extend this short loop hike with some eastward exploration toward Ragged Top, using only the old jeep road. It is critical in Ironwood Forest National Monument never to trailblaze above the old mining road skirting Ragged Top; always stay on the road or below it—the land higher up is a sensitive lambing area for bighorn sheep.

To get back to the trailhead, head down the road due west; you will go through a gate at just beyond the 1-mile mark. Close the gate behind you and continue along the road all the way to your trailhead.

THE WHITE MOUNTAINS

71. South Fork

Round trip: 6 miles
Hiking time: 3 hours
Difficulty: easy
High point: 8188 feet
Elevation change: 668 feet
Best: March through November
Maps: Greer and Eagar USGS
Contact: Apache-Sitgreaves National Forest, Springerville Ranger
Station, (928) 333-4372

Getting there: From Springerville, take State Hwy 260 west toward Show Low for approximately 5 miles. Turn left onto County Road 4124 (south; also called Forest Road 560). Follow the road to its end and park at the trailhead, toward the back of the campground. You will see a sign for campground fees; day hikers do not pay a fee to park at the trailhead. After your dog is watered and leashed, head out from the kiosk at the trailhead going south.

The name of South Fork Trail 97 refers to the south fork of the Little Colorado River, a perennial stream flowing through the mixed conifer- and

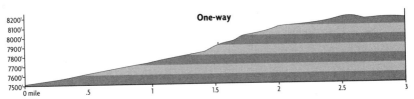

aspen-lined meadows of eastern Arizona's White Mountains. The pockets of aspens, along with the occasional cottonwood, sycamore, and Gambel oak at the streamside, add autumn's russets and golds to this pretty, evergreen landscape.

You and your dog are exploring this area along a narrow footpath that is a very comfortable compacted forest floor almost the entire way. The trail never winds far from the banks of the river, and there are many places where

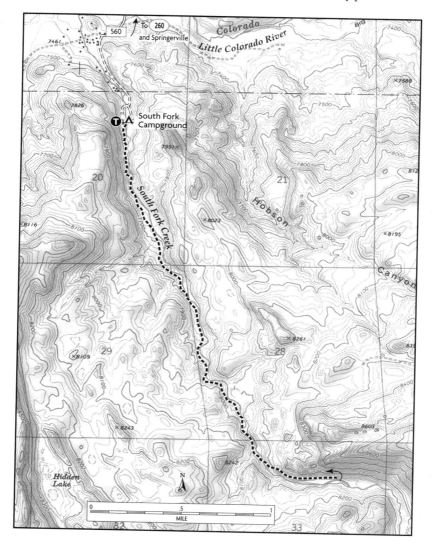

An open mixed-conifer and aspen forest shades your creekside ramble with Fido along the South Fork Trail.

your dog can cool her pads; remember to purify any water you take to drink.

The path takes you upstream and uphill, initially in shade, on a very gentle grade. A meadow pours out of the forest at 0.5 mile, and for a time you and your dog are traversing a sunny expanse of grasses and wildflowers. You duck under shade again soon enough, and at 1 mile pass a tiny spring to the right of the trail, tucked under a shelf of land.

At just past the halfway point to the terminus, 1.7 miles, there are a number of terrific break places in shade or flat areas by the stream. You shortly cross a forest road and continue your southeast heading to pick up the path. There is a trail junction at the 2-mile mark; the leftward path departs from the stream (yet is still technically the South Fork Trail) and heads to Mexican Hay Lake.

Your path stays with the Little Colorado along a fishing trail that continues south (forward) for just under 1 mile. The path narrows further and the area has a wilder feel. Huge boulders preside over the trail. You cross a tributary of the river at 2.1 miles just below a beaver dam. Quickly, the path fades to barely more than a thin line separating blades of grass. Have faith though and keep heading southeast here to cross the river at 2.25 miles (the river will now be on your right). The footpath still has good and frequent access to the river, but is now more brambly. Poison oak crops up occasionally, so watch that your dog doesn't nose it and then give you a sloppy kiss. Ferns pop up here and there along your way—remind Fido not to graze.

You go through a gate and continue on the still climbing and somewhat rockier path. The path bends east after crossing the river. The trail winds in and out of the floodplain, climbing the canyon walls for a time, then dropping back down into meadow. Soon you cross another tributary, this one bubbling down from your left at 2.75 miles—enjoy the splash break. Just past the 3-mile mark it is time to turn the leash around and enjoy a pleasant, easy downhill stroll back the way you came.

72. Indian Spring Loop

Round trip: 7.5 miles
Hiking time: 4 hours
Difficulty: easy
High point: 9075 feet
Elevation change: 500 feet
Best: April through November
Maps: Big Lake South USGS
Contact: Apache-Sitgreaves National Forest, Springerville Ranger Station, (928) 333-4372
Map: Road not maintained November through April; check conditions before setting out.

Getting there: To get there from Springerville, take State Hwy 260 west approximately 4.5 miles to the junction with Hwy 261 and turn left.

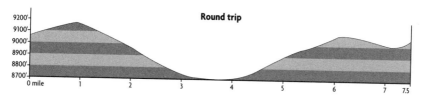

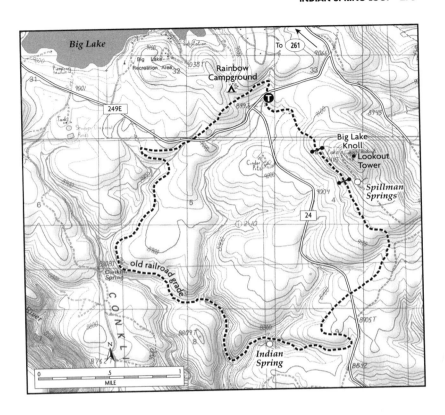

Continue for about 16 miles altogether—you will stay left at the junction with Hwy 273; here, Hwy 261 is also known as Forest Road 113 (though it is not clearly signed as such). The pavement ends and the road turns into FR 249. In about 0.7 mile, take a right onto FR 249E. It is 0.4 mile to the trailhead, which is on your left, at the small parking lot.

After watering and leashing your dog, from the kiosk head south. In this Mexican gray wolf recovery country, bears also abound, so follow the leash rules for your dog's safety. Pack in additional water in case the springs are dry, and purify what you take if water is flowing. On Indian Spring Trail 627 you and your dog first trek through a lovely meadow lined with firs and ponderosa pines; soon, you are under their broad canopies and enjoying the wide path and shade. This hiking- and biking-only loop trail swells and dips, giving you and Fido an easy but very pleasant and generally shady and cool workout. If you want a more remote experience, avoid weekends between Memorial Day and Labor Day, when this trail occasionally sees heavy use.

Your trail winds south, then southeast, and you make a modest elevation gain as you approach Big Lake Knoll. Just before you get to a turn-off to the Big Lake Lookout Tower at 0.5 mile, you will cross the first of two wooden cattle guards; the slats are just far enough apart on these structures that small dogs will have to be carried over and large dogs carefully passed under the fences. Add approximately half a mile—this is a steep side trip—onto your hike to get a great panoramic view of the forest. The lookout trail takes off uphill to the left; if you want to continue on the Indian Spring loop, just head south (straight) at the junction. Just past the second cattle guard, at 0.9 mile, you come to Spillman Springs, captured and flowing through quaint, hollowed-log troughs installed by the Civilian Conservation Corps, that would not have been out of place in an episode of "Gilligan's Island."

Beautiful boulders and towering outcroppings squat on the forest

A rare flock of ferns along the Indian Spring Loop

floor. Past 1 mile, you and your dog pass through a little patch of ferns—
no unauthorized trail treats here! This is a chatty part of the forest in
springtime, with birdcalls shouted down from the thick canopy. A beautiful grove of aspens casts a luminous glow at the 1.3-mile mark as the
trail turns eastward along the loop, before heading south again (and
gently downhill) to Indian Spring. You cross FR 24 at 1.9 miles—trail
markers guide you here, though the footpath is quite easy to find after
the crossing.

At 2.25 miles, just before you enter the territory around Indian Spring,
you trek through a spot of Seussical whimsy where trees are misshapen, their
trunks strangely bowed. Also, you come upon gargantuan aspens—their
eminence a sign not just of their age but a reminder that water is close. Take
your pick of shady spots here for a rest and water break—your trek through
the meadows is quite exposed for a time.

The trail approaches the sprawling complex of meadows leading to
Indian Spring just as it joins up with an old road. There are trail markers here—at 2.5 miles—guiding you through this funky merger, where
your path turns west. The meadows attract elk, birds, and bears, so if
you have your field glasses, now is a good time to make them handy.
The path, which has been composed largely of a comfortable and fairly
soft forest floor, narrows now and is covered with cinders. Just beyond
a screen of trees at 3 miles, look to the left—chances are, your dog will
have sniffed out the water already—to see Indian Spring and its related
ponds, if the water is flowing. A sign helps identify the area if the water is not flowing.

The loop trail continues past the spring, first jogging southward, then
northwest, to join up with an old railroad grade, formerly the Apache
Railway Company's Maverick Line, which operated through the early
1970s. You and your dog follow a gentle climb along this portion of the
loop. At 5.5 miles is a trail junction with the West Fork Trail 628; continue northeast (right) to stay on the Indian Spring Loop.

Shortly, you dip under the cool, evergreen canopy again, but only briefly,
so enjoy this shady area with your pooch before continuing on. More lush
meadows are in store for you and your dog, and the wildflowers are showy
throughout spring and summer. After you cross FR 249E, your last trail
segment is a rolling path near Rainbow Campground; continue northeast
when you come to the junction of the campground spur trail. At 7.3 miles,
your trail turns right (south) and crosses FR 249E again, leading you and
your dog back to the trailhead.

APPENDIX: RESOURCES

Reference books

Mullally, Linda. *Hiking with Dogs: Becoming a Wilderness-Wise Dog Owner.* Missoula, MT: Falcon Guides, 1999.

Smith, Cheryl S. *On the Trail with Your Canine Companion: Getting the Most out of Hiking and Camping with Your Dog.* New York: Howell Book House, 1996.

McConnell, Patricia B., Ph.D. *The Other End of the Leash: Why We Do What We Do Around Dogs.* New York: Ballantine, 2002.

Acker, Randy, DVM. *Dog First Aid: A Field Guide to Emergency Care for the Outdoor Dog.* Gallatin Gateway, MT: Wilderness Adventure Press, 1999.

Pet First Aid: Quick Guide to Animal Emergencies. Ruffwear Flip Book. (available at *www.ruffwear.com*).

Courses and other information

The American Red Cross offers Pet First-Aid and CPR, Human First-Aid, Wilderness First-Aid, and many more helpful courses for outdoor enthusiasts.

Arizona chapters can now be reached via a single website at *www.arizona redcross.org,* or by calling:
Northern District, (928) 779-5494
Central District, (602) 336-6660
Southern Arizona Chapter, (520) 318-6740

Humane Society chapters offer a Pet CPR and First-Aid Class. For details, go to *www.azhumane.org* or call (602) 997-7586, Ext. 1024, in Phoenix, and (520) 321-3704, in Tucson.

The Maricopa County Parks Department offers ranger-led safety programs at most of their park locations. Topics range from desert survival and edible plants to land navigation and recognizing venomous creatures. They regularly schedule snake aversion courses as well. Go to *www.maricopa.gov/ parks* for more information, or call a county park near you.

Similar classes are offered through the City of Phoenix Parks Department. Visit *www.ci.phoenix.az.us/PARKS/hikemain.html* for more information, or call the Phoenix Mountain Preserve office at (602) 262-7901.

The American Society for the Prevention of Cruelty to Animals (ASPCA) Animal Poison Control Center is available to answer questions pertaining to ingested poisons 24 hours a day, 7 days a week, by calling (888) 426-4435 toll free; general information is also available on their web site, *www.apcc.aspca.org.*

Gear

For basics like backpacks, water bowls, and first-aid kits, as well as luxury items such as gourmet trail treats, check out these manufacturers' products online:

www.granitegear.com
www.ruffwear.com
www.planetdog.com

INDEX

ABOUT THE AUTHOR

Renée Guillory is a correspondent for the *Arizona Daily Sun*. She also writes for the Grand Canyon Chapter of the Sierra Club, where she has been an active member since 1993. She supports the Canine Hiking Club of Arizona as well. Renée hikes with her trail-hardy Husky-mutt mix, Sparky, and with her Akita-Collie-mutt mix, Artemis, who has taken to the trail splendidly. Renée has hiked, backpacked, and camped with her dogs in Arizona for more than a decade and is an expert on hiking in Arizona's hot weather. She is passionate about helping the area's new residents and tourists to be more savvy on timing and preparation for fun, safe outdoor activity in Arizona's extreme climate and rugged landscape.

THE MOUNTAINEERS, founded in 1906, is a nonprofit outdoor activity and conservation club, whose mission is "to explore, study, preserve, and enjoy the natural beauty of the outdoors. . . . " Based in Seattle, Washington, the club is now the third-largest such organization in the United States, with seven branches throughout Washington State.

The Mountaineers sponsors both classes and year-round outdoor activities in the Pacific Northwest, which include hiking, mountain climbing, ski-touring, snowshoeing, bicycling, camping, kayaking and canoeing, nature study, sailing, and adventure travel. The club's conservation division supports environmental causes through educational activities, sponsoring legislation, and presenting informational programs. All club activities are led by skilled, experienced volunteers, who are dedicated to promoting safe and responsible enjoyment and preservation of the outdoors.

If you would like to participate in these organized outdoor activities or the club's programs, consider a membership in The Mountaineers. For information and an application, write or call The Mountaineers, Club Headquarters, 300 Third Avenue West, Seattle, Washington 98119; 206-284-6310.

The Mountaineers Books, an active, nonprofit publishing program of the club, produces guidebooks, instructional texts, historical works, natural history guides, and works on environmental conservation. All books produced by The Mountaineers fulfill the club's mission.

Send or call for our catalog of more than 500 outdoor titles:

The Mountaineers Books
1001 SW Klickitat Way, Suite 201
Seattle, WA 98134
800-553-4453
mbooks@mountaineersbooks.org
www.mountaineersbooks.org

The Mountaineers Books is proud to be a corporate sponsor of The Leave No Trace Center for Outdoor Ethics, whose mission is to promote and inspire responsible outdoor recreation through education, research, and partnerships. The Leave No Trace program is focused specifically on human-powered (nonmotorized) recreation.

Leave No Trace strives to educate visitors about the nature of their recreational impacts, as well as offer techniques to prevent and minimize such impacts. Leave No Trace is best understood as an educational and ethical program, not as a set of rules and regulations.

For more information, visit *www.LNT.org,* or call 800-332-4100.

OTHER TITLES YOU MIGHT ENJOY FROM
THE MOUNTAINEERS BOOKS

Desert Sense: Camping, Hiking, and Biking in Hot, Dry Climates, *Bruce Grubbs*
How to make your way safely in the desert, no matter what your mode of travel.

Don't Forget the Duct Tape: Tips and Tricks for Repairing Outdoor Gear
Kristin Hostetter
Pack this little guide with you and be an outdoor fixit guru!

Digital Photography Outdoors: A Field Guide for Travel & Adventure Photographers, *James Martin*
Special techniques for outdoor adventure shooting—making the most of digital's advantages.

Lightning Strikes: Staying Safe Under Stormy Skies, *Jeff Renner*
A quick, highly informative read for anyone who spends time in the outdoors.

Best Loop Hikes: Arizona
Bruce Grubbs
Don't hike the same path twice—here's the first book devoted to loop trails in Arizona.

ALSO IN THE BEST HIKES WITH DOGS SERIES . . .

Western Washington,
Dan A. Nelson
Oregon, *Ellen Morris Bishop*
Inland Northwest,
Craig Romano &
Alan L. Bauer

Available at fine bookstores and outdoor stores, by phone at 800-553-4453 or on the web at *www.mountaineersbooks.org.*

THE MOUNTAINEERS BOOKS